OUR PRACTICES
OUR SELVES

TODD MAY

OUR PRACTICES
OUR SELVES

Or, What It Means to Be Human

THE PENNSYLVANIA STATE UNIVERSITY PRESS
UNIVERSITY PARK, PENNSYLVANIA

LIBRARY OF CONGRESS CATALOGING-IN-PUBLICATION DATA

May, Todd, 1955–

Our practices, our selves, or, What it means to be human / Todd May.

p.   cm.

Includes bibliographical references and index.

ISBN 0-271-02085-7 (cloth : alk. paper)

ISBN 0-271-02086-5 (pbk. : alk. paper)

1. Practice (Philosophy).   2. Philosophical anthropology.   I. Title:
Our practices, our selves.   II. Title: What it means to be human.
III. Title.

B831.3.M332 2001
128—dc21

00-032367

It is the policy of The Pennsylvania State University Press to use acid-free paper
for the first printing of all clothbound books. Publications on uncoated stock
satisfy the minimum requirements of American National Standard for Information
Sciences—Permanence of Paper for Printed Library Materials, ANSI Z39.48–
1992.

C O N T E N T S

ACKNOWLEDGMENTS

When I began to study philosophy back in college, I did so with the goal of coming to understand who I was and how I should live. Gradually, as I became familiar with the intricacies of philosophical debate, I shifted my focus toward more abstract philosophical argumentation. Looking back, it seems to me that that shift was a necessary moment in my own philosophical development—but for many of us in philosophy, that kind of argumentation becomes an end in itself rather than a means by which we can grapple with the big questions. This book, then, marks a return of sorts to the themes and preoccupations that fed my interest in philosophy. Although the book is informed by the abstractions that have passed my way over the past twenty-five years, it focuses on trying to answer (in a nontechnical way) the important philosophical question of who we are.

A number of people have been generous enough to offer a critical reading of the manuscript. In particular, I would like to thank Jennifer Alt, Dan Conway, Garry Hagberg, Tim Holsopple, and

Ladelle McWhorter for their helpful comments. In addition, Laura
Reed-Morrisson's editing greatly improved the style and tone of the
manuscript. Cherene Holland, Steve Kress, and Patty Mitchell at Penn
State Press have, as usual, been a pleasure to work with.

My greatest debt is to Sandy Thatcher. He first encouraged me to
write this book, and he saw it through (and kept my spirits up) in the
face of its doubters. Sandy has always believed in the importance of
philosophy, and displayed that belief time and again during the evolution of *Our Practices, Our Selves*.

1 OUR PRACTICES

THINKING ABOUT PRACTICES

This is a book about who we are.

It is often said that in this historical period large questions like "Who am I?" or "Who are we?" are no longer relevant to people. Questions like these, and the people who try to answer them, are relics from an earlier era. A lack of time, an overabundance of diversions, a hyperspecialization in our knowledge—all of these lead us to no longer care or think about such crucial questions. Rather than search for some sense of ourselves and of the meaning of our existence, we try instead to work pragmatically with what presents itself to us, cobbling together the most comfortable or satisfying or lucrative lives we can.

I believe that those who say this are mistaken. Yes, many of us are squeezed for time in a world that moves more quickly than it used to, and yes, there are lots of diversions, and yes again, specialization does take its toll on broad types of reflection. But if we look around us, the evidence for people's trying to make sense of themselves is everywhere. Who doesn't wonder whether there is a God and, if there is, what relation to God one might have? (The number of books published on religion has skyrocketed in recent years.) Who doesn't stop at periods in one's life and ask oneself whether *this* is the person one really is or really wants to be? What teenager does not assess the character of his or her future at least partly in terms of what the previous generation has made of itself? And what parents, watching their children grow up, are not forced to reflect on what they have made of themselves?

If it seems as though the questions of "Who am I?" and "Who are we?" are not as visible as they might be, this is not so much because the questions are distant from us, but because they are so close that it is as easy to miss them as it is to forget that we're breathing. In approaching the question of who we are, then, what I want to do is not to drag you into some foreign land, but to pause over a matter that haunts us all throughout our lives.

The question of who we are—at least as I want to ask it—is a question about each of us individually and about us in our being together. But it's not a question about *we* as in "we Americans," or *we* as in "we inhabitants of the late twentieth century," or *we* as in "we *Homo sapiens*." It's also not a question about *we* in the way that many recent theorists of multicultural identity have asked it (a point I'll return to near the end of the book). It's about we as in who each of us is, and who we are in our various groupings: who you are and who I am and who each of these other folks we share the planet with is. It is a question that this book will try to say something worthwhile about, something that will help us understand ourselves and our place in the world. And, as you may have already guessed, the punch line is going to run something like "we are our practices."

What this book proposes to do, then, is to use the concept of practices in order to provide an answer to the question of who we are.

My own philosophical approach in this book will be to *start* with some fairly obvious and pedestrian observations and to try to show how a proper investigation of those observations may lead us to see ourselves differently. (This, by the way, is not an uncommon way to philosophize, although the temptation often is to move from the obvious to the obscure.) There is much that we tend to gloss over in our everyday lives. We see things, recognize them as obvious, and then move on. After all, one can't linger over everything that drifts by (or, more often these days, races by)—unless, of course, one is a philosopher. And even then, one can only linger over some of the things that drift or race by. But by picking the right things to linger over and lingering over them in the right way, sometimes one can learn something important or solve an intellectual puzzle that one had not known how to solve before. So it is, I think, with practices. They are among the things that seem self-evident to us but that are worth lingering over.

What I would like to show is that by understanding the role that practices play in our lives, we can learn much about what we do, how we think about ourselves and our world, and why we sometimes find ourselves in the intellectual dilemmas that confront us. My hope is that if I string enough pedestrian truths about our practices together in the right way, a picture of who we are will begin to emerge that is a picture worth having. And to be able to present a picture of ourselves worth having is, it seems to me, one of the important tasks of philosophy.

Let me issue a word of caution, however, about what exactly I am going to claim for my picture. Philosophy is often thought of, by philosophers and nonphilosophers alike, as a discipline that dictates its truths from on high. It is as though philosophy stood outside our day-to-day world, seeing it from a vantage point far removed from the practices in which we engage. Given the approach that I propose to take, such a view of philosophy—and of the philosophical picture I will try to sketch here—would be mistaken. Although I will talk at length about the status of claims people make when I get to the second chapter of this book, let me say something here about the status of my own claims.

Philosophy, I would argue, is a practice, and in that sense, it is similar to many other practices I'll discuss in this book. Like civil engineering or psychology or history, it does not come to its findings by disengaging itself from the world but instead by engaging the world in its own particular way. When I make a philosophical claim—or design an entire philosophical picture—I am not drawing on secret or indubitable or arcane truths that are immune to critical scrutiny by my readers. Instead, the picture I create will be convincing, if it is convincing, because it can find its place in a larger picture (or set of pictures) of the world that we all share. In other words, my philosophical claim about who we are is meant to convince you not *in spite* of many of the things you already believe but *because* of them.

This is not to say that philosophy doesn't ever change the way in which we see things. Really good philosophy often does change the way in which we see things. But when it does, it does so because it makes *better* sense of some aspect of the world or of ourselves than our previous ways of seeing things did, and is therefore convincing to us on grounds that we can accept—or at least should be able to accept, if we think hard enough about the matter.

That said, and before turning to the idea of practices, let me reflect for a moment on the question that this book tries to answer: the question of who we are. It is a question that can be asked in many ways, partly depending on the "we" in question and on the kind of answer one hopes to find. Regarding the "we," the group I have in mind is *people*. And by people, I mean, at least for the most part, human beings. If it turns out that dolphins or chimpanzees are like us in so many ways that we want to broaden the class of people to include them, then my guess is that among the things that dolphins or chimpanzees do that makes them so much like us is that they are largely formed in who they are by their participation in practices. I won't argue for that point. But if this book is compelling about practices, the idea that engagement in practices is required for "personhood" should be at least initially plausible.

The other issue tied up with the question of who we are—what kind of answer we hope to find—is a little more complicated. Are we looking for a biological explanation of what makes people people? Or do we seek some essence of the human soul or mind? Is theology an appropriate approach to the question, or should we restrict ourselves to more naturalistic explanations? Are we trying to *explain* something?

And what about the possibility that there is no one thing that makes people who they are?

Before tipping my hand on some of the questions I've just raised, let me concede right away that I don't imagine that there is any one thing that makes people who they are. If there is a single most important thing, it is most likely either the practices we participate in—and are subject to—or our genetic makeup. (And who knows about this latter possibility?) But in the end, although a variety of factors may play significant (or less significant) roles, it is probably their interaction that makes us the people we are. To look for the single factor that explains who people are as people is like looking for the single factor that explains France's winning the World Cup or the appeal of the sitcom *Seinfeld*. My claim on behalf of practices, then, isn't that they explain everything, but that they explain and help us understand a lot of what it is like to be who we are. And, as we'll see, part of the appeal of the idea of practices is that it offers a framework within which we can interpret the roles of a number of other factors that contribute to making people who they—we—are.

But if I'm not looking for a single answer to or explanation of this puzzle, what am I looking for? What kind of account will answer the question of who we are? Traditionally, there are two kinds of accounts that try to answer questions like this: one called *explanation,* and the other, *understanding*. Proponents of explanation as a response to philosophical questions tend to be more impressed with science, especially natural science, and tend to seek causal answers for questions like "Who are we?" For them, a biological account of genetic makeup, perhaps coupled with a reference to environmental reinforcement, might make a nice answer to such a question. Explainers are not likely to be sympathetic to answers that seek to give us a hard-to-articulate sense of understanding, which they see as empty poetry rather than legitimate intellectual work.

There is much of value in the project of explanation. Its virtues coincide generally with those of science. No mysterious entities are invoked (or at least none that don't hook up in some recognizable way to nonmysterious entities), potential answers are to a great degree falsifiable, and you don't need any particular theological commitments to accept them. Much of the progress science has made has been due to its emphasis on explanation and particularly on causal explanation.

However, in addressing the question of who we are, not just any explanation—even if it is true—will do. A physicist, for example, could tell us a story of who each of us is that would involve our accepting nothing more than the idea of atoms and basic physical forces. It would be a true story. But it would not be very satisfying, because when we ask about who we are, we are generally seeking something more than just some explanation of our bodies' atoms. We want something that gives us a sense of ourselves as beings who have goals, form relationships, experience emotion, and reflect on our lives. As some put it, we seek *understanding*.

Understanders, as opposed to explainers, are more impressed by the sense of intellectual grasp that an account of something, like an account of who we are, gives us. It is often hard to say what constitutes that sense of intellectual grasp. But there are many things that are difficult to articulate, although we know them when we encounter them. For instance, I can't for the life of me tell you in any but the broadest terms what makes a good jazz tune a good one; when I hear John Coltrane play, though, I know that I'm in the presence of superior jazz. Now I may be stretching a point here. Music, after all, is always hard to render in language, more so than accounts of who we are, which are already offered in language. Fair enough. But among competing accounts of who we are, some may seem better to us not merely because they converge well with science but also because they respond to our sense of who we are, a sense that is often difficult to put into words. Even if they deny that we are who we sense we are, as existentialist accounts did in the 1940s and 1950s, they still reach us in a way that is meaningful to us, that seems to address (if not lay to rest) the concerns that motivate us—even when we can't say exactly what those concerns are.

The worry that follows understanders is that they may be ready to embrace accounts of who we are that satisfy some deep sense of intellectual grasp but are just wrong. For my money, Freud's view is a good example of a satisfyingly wrong account of who we are. Psychoanalytic accounts are very seductive. They have mystery, they give a person depth, they're often tragic, and they allow for a project of self-discovery and even personal growth, more or less. The problem is that they're slippery in several important ways. Psychoanalytic accounts are hard to verify or falsify. They don't necessarily accord well with other scientific findings. And often the accounts of psychoanalysts seem a bit circular. (I suspect, although I won't argue for this, that everything that is right in Freud is in Proust's *Remembrance of Things Past,* and that if it's not there but it is in Freud, then it's wrong.)

It may sound as though I'm trying to say that there is a gulf between explaining and understanding, but I'm not. I don't want to leave the impression that a good explanation cannot be satisfying or that an account that offers understanding never explains anything. Rather, the trick in trying to answer (or, as I have now admitted, partially answer) the question of who we are is to do both at the same time. One needs to offer an account of who we are that both explains many aspects of ourselves—and does so in ways that are consistent with current scientific theory—and still gives us that sense of intellectual grasp that characterizes understanding.

This does not seem to me to be an impossible task. Einstein offered an account of the universe that is both explanatory and intellectually satisfying. Darwin offered an account of species change that is both explanatory and (to many of us) intellectually satisfying. What I am attempting here is, of course, of a much lower intellectual order than what Einstein and Darwin achieved. But as their examples show, there doesn't seem to be any reason to assume at the outset that in approaching large and difficult questions—such as the question of who we are—we will be forced to choose between explanation and understanding.

Not that I think that an account of ourselves in terms of practices will satisfy everyone. On the explanatory side, those inclined to what has come to be called *physicalism*—the view that any successful account of ourselves (or anything else) must be couched in terms of physics—will find my approach wanting. After all, I'll be talking about people, goals, societies, language, and power; none of these are terms used in physicalist explanations. On the understanding side, those who hold that all accounts of who we are must ultimately be theologically grounded will not be too happy with my emphasis on the centrality of practices. God does not put in an appearance here, although church-going does. However, there is nothing I will say in this book that is incompatible with a broad theological framework.

In the rest of this chapter, I plan to say a bit about what a practice is, begin to discuss why the concept of practices is important in thinking about who we are, and contrast practices with other related social entities, specifically communities, civil societies, and cultures. Then, in the next two chapters, I'll expand on the importance of practices to who we are by discussing the relationships between knowledge and practices and between morality, politics, and practices. In the end, I hope to make plausible the idea that our knowledge, our morality, and much of our political life is best understood—at least currently—in terms of social practices.

PRACTICES

If I'm going to make the case that who we are is largely a matter of our practices, the first thing I'll need to do is get clear on the nature of a practice. Without that clarity, it will be easy to call too many different types of things practices, which won't offer any real insight into who we are.

Okay, so what is a practice?

A *practice,* as I will be using the term, can be defined in this way: "a regularity (or regularities) of behavior, usually goal-directed, that is socially normatively governed." In order to understand what that means, let me expand a bit on the three aspects of that defini-tion. First, goal-directedness. Most practices have some aim in view. Teaching, for instance, is a practice that has as its goal the imparting of knowledge to students. There may be teachers who don't care about their students' knowledge; nevertheless, the practice of teaching itself is characterized by that goal. Cleaning is a practice that has as its goal the removal of dirt. (And I don't know anyone who engages in that practice who doesn't have that goal in mind.) Children playing base-ball are engaged in a practice, although children running aimlessly around a playground are not—and I take it that no one thinks of them as engaged in some sort of practice.

However, there can be instances of practices that do not have an end in view. While staring off into space is not a practice, sitting Zen, which (at least according to its proponents) has no aim in view, is a practice. Such goal-less practices, I believe, are the exception rather than the rule. They do seem to exist, however.

Now, someone might take issue with such exceptions to practices having a goal. He or she might argue that in the case of sitting Zen, for instance, there is a goal in view: that of achieving oneness with the universe, or *satori*. If it were true that all practices had some aim in view, I wouldn't mind that at all, because it would make the definition simpler and more clear-cut. But I'm just not sure that the simplification works. It seems to me to be fudging the Zen example to add a goal to it. I'm no expert on Zen, but practitioners of it tell me that you really do have to lose all sense of goal-directedness in order to achieve *satori*, and that *satori* is, in a sense, not a goal but the absence of goals. It is a state of goal-lessness. Here someone might say, "Aha. Then Zen does have a goal. Its goal is the state of goal-lessness." While that may be true, to incorporate goal-lessness into the category of goals threatens to undo the idea of goals altogether. It's like saying that all practices are goal-directed, which means that all practices have some goal in view, even if that goal is no goal at all. I'm not sure that embracing that paradox (though isn't it part of the practice of Zen to involve us in paradoxes?) is any better than just admitting that although almost all practices have goals, there may be some that don't.

The second aspect of my definition of practices also needs exploring: that is, the idea of social normative governance. This is more complex. A practice must, in order to be a practice, be socially and normatively governed. I don't want to say "rule-governed," since there need not be explicit rules governing all of the behaviors in question. However, although there may not be explicit rules, there will at least be "know-how" about how the practice is performed. There are right ways and wrong ways of engaging in the practice; though not all of the participants may be able to articulate exactly what it is that makes the right way right, they know it when they see it. (The people who can articulate what is right and wrong about various aspects of a practice are often thought of as the experts in that practice.) When teaching one's kid how to ride a bike, for instance, one may find oneself saying something like, "When the bike goes this way, do *this*," where *this* is some sort of twist of the body. The same goes for many practices that involve subtle bodily posturings, such as dance and the martial arts.

The normative governance of practices must also be a social one. In other words, there is no such thing as a practice that can only be for one specific person. If I invent a game that only I can play, because only I can know the game's norms, then I have not invented a practice. In that sense, practices involve what might be called *roles,* or normatively governed places in which people engage in the practice. Roles can be fulfilled by any number of people. They are not reserved for specific individuals. But in order for there to be roles, the norms of those roles must be masterable by (or at least understandable to) others. Not everyone can play every role, of course, and there will be practices that require enough expertise that very few people can play *any* of the roles. But in order for there to be a practice, there cannot be norms that only one individual can know. In that case, rather than having a practice, you would have a personal fantasy or a private game.

One might even go further here and argue that there can't be a personal fantasy or game like that. The reason for this is that in order to have such a fantasy or game, one would at least have to formulate the rules of the game (if not all the norms, recalling that not all norms are rules) in language. And for those norms that are not formulable into rules, there must be some fact of the matter about right and wrong ways of doing things. That's what makes them norms. Now, inasmuch as a linguistic formulation of rules is required, and since languages can be learned by others, it would seem that others could also learn the rules of the game. As for the other norms, it would seem that one could learn to distinguish correct and incorrect ways of doing things, just as one learns to distinguish right and wrong ways of bicycle riding, dancing, and the martial arts. And if others could learn the rules and the other norms of this personal fantasy or game, then the fantasy or game would no longer be personal. It would have roles that could be filled by others, and thus would become a practice.

(This line of argument is a simplified version of the argument offered by the philosopher Ludwig Wittgenstein that there is no such thing as a private language.)

The social normative governance of a practice does not entail that the practice itself must be socially performed. Even though the norms are social, the activity itself does not have to be. Diary writing, for instance, is a solitary activity. It is both socially and normatively governed, however. There are ways in which one writes diaries: types of topics that are considered, potential readers (if even only oneself) that are kept in mind, and the like. These norms are socially recognized as constitutive of the practice of diary writing. If one does not conform to them, one cannot be said to be engaged in an instance of the practice of diary writing.

Some may worry about the social aspect of the normative governance of practices. Is it really the case that what is to count as a practice must be capable of being socially recognized as one (not necessarily by everyone, of course, but by those who can be expected to recognize such practices)? Doesn't this lead to some kind of totalitarianism of the social, in the sense that what one does is worthwhile only if the society in which the act occurs recognizes it as worthwhile?

You can see how such a worry would arise. We Western types like our individual freedom. We like to think that in matters of importance to us, each of us gets some say in how things should go. We like to think that our individual desires and projects are not merely fodder to feed larger social goals. Particularly in the United States, people are leery of submitting the individual to the social; it smacks of certain political theories that many would rather believe dead and buried. However, in my view, a practice requires socially recognizable norms. So it would seem that somehow the individual is being subsumed into the social in an objectionable way, that individual desires get their legitimacy only in connection with socially recognized norms. Is that so?

I don't believe that it is. The point in isolating the concept of practices is not to tell people how to act. It is not to tell them how their lives should and should not go. There is no implicit commitment here to the idea that practices are good and behaviors that aren't engagements in instances of practices are bad, or that individuals *ought* to engage in practices rather than not engage in them. (As this book unfolds, we should begin to see that such engagement is both inevitable and largely constitutive of who individuals are. But that's a different issue, an issue about what we are like rather than about who we should be.) Some practices—for example, political organizing in solidarity with the oppressed, volunteering at soup kitchens, or contributing money to worthy causes—are good; other practices, such as political torture or scamming the elderly with bogus insurance protection, are bad.

What I am getting at here is not a theory or some kind of recipe for how to act, but an approach—ultimately, the proper approach to one of the most significant contributing factors to who we are. This approach requires that we reject the idea of the individual as a kind of self-enclosed entity. But it equally requires that we move away from the alternative that is so often offered: individuals as products of some vast social force, like the nation or society or capitalism (although I will have something to say about the latter near the end of the book). It requires something in between those perspectives—that something being a practice.

The concept of a practice, then, lies at the intersection of the individual and the social. The social aspect of the concept—the social nature of a practice's normative governance—does not force us to take any normative stand *pro* or *contra* practices, and it does not give the members of a society any special power in delegating to its members the say-so over what are and are not practices. It merely tries to allow us to discover the point at which practices are social. There need be no worry that the requirement that practices be socially recognized will carry any insidious dangers in its wake.

So far, we have looked at two characteristics of practices: their goal-directedness and their social normative governance. The third characteristic that I want to address is that practices involve regularities of behavior. In order for something to be a practice, the various people engaged in it must be able to be said to be "doing the same thing" under some reasonable description of their behavior. What constitutes a reasonable description in a given situation can be a matter of debate; we can begin to see the pitfalls that might threaten attempts at description when we recognize that, with suitably abstract wording, people we would want to say are engaged in very different practices can be said to be doing the same thing. For instance, a person handing a letter to a postal clerk and a person holding up that same postal clerk can be said to be doing the same thing under the description "interacting with a postal clerk." But we would surely want to say that mailing letters and robbing post offices involve two different practices.

I will not address that problem here, because for a couple of reasons I don't think that it affects the general thrust of the account. First, I don't want to deny that practices can be composed of other practices, so the general issue of the level of abstraction does not introduce any particular problems. Second, I don't see any reason to deny that practices have fuzzy borders: it is difficult to say at what point someone who is marginally involved in a practice passes over into not being involved with it. This fuzziness is not a defect of the account but a fact about practices. As regularities, practices allow for variation in the kinds of behavior that can be considered part of the regularity; those variations, in turn, often need to be assessed in particular cases in order to say whether someone is involved in a given practice. A person who attends a church by walking slowly up the church steps can be said to be engaged in the same practice as the person who attends a church by bounding up the steps. But how about the person who stands in the doorway and half-listens to the sermon? This is a matter for deliberation, not because practices are not regularities, but because it is not always clear what variations on behavior count as being within the range of a specific regularity.

That said, however, there is still a clarification that needs to be made. In practices, the regularities that different people are engaged in may not be *identical* but *complementary*. In other words, what makes up the regularities of the practice is usually not that people perform the same acts but that they perform different, complementary acts that mesh into a whole. For instance, in baseball there are often at least ten people on the field at the same time (not including managers, umpires, people in the dugout, and others). They are all engaged in the practice of playing baseball, and indeed are all engaged in the same instance of that practice. However, they are not all "doing the same thing" in the sense of displaying the same regularity. Each of the roles assumed by the players is socially and normatively governed, and each involves its own regularities. Taken together, those regularities are complementary; they constitute that instance of the practice of playing baseball. Thus, we need to understand the regularities of a practice as being either regularities of identity or regularities of complementarity.

Having just offered this word of clarification, let me offer another word of clarification, in order to clarify the clarification I just made. (It's stuff like this that allows philosophers to enjoy the reputation we currently possess.) In the last paragraph, I said that the regularities within a practice don't have to be regularities of identity but can be regularities of complementarity. That is, the players in the baseball game don't have to be doing the same thing—they're not all pitching—but can be doing complementary things—pitching, fielding, batting, and the like. A couple of paragraphs before that one, I talked about the difficulty of determining when people are doing the same thing in the sense of being engaged in the same practice— the letter depositor and the robber. I just want to be clear here that those two discussions of "the same thing" are distinct. In the case of regularities, what I mean by doing "the same thing" is "engaged in identical behavior." My point there was that *within* a given practice, people don't have to be doing the same thing, i.e., exhibiting identical behavior. Not everybody in a baseball game has to be pitching in order to be involved in the same practice. Before that, in discussing whether two disparate types of behavior can be classified as belonging to the same practice, I was asking about whether two seemingly distinct practices—mailing a letter and robbing a post office—could be classified as instances of the same practice.

So now we have in hand an idea of what is meant by the crucial terms used in the definition of a practice. In addition to the three characteristics of a practice cited in the definition, there is a fourth characteristic that practices possess, one that does not appear in the definition but is entailed by it. We have already seen this fourth characteristic in connection with the discussion of the social normative governance of practices. Practices are discursive, by which I mean that they involve the use of language. It is easy to see why practices must be discursive. Since practices are socially normatively governed, they require some sort of communication between participants in order to learn or to coordinate the activities that that practice involves. (This does not imply that all the norms of a practice must be articulable by each participant in the practice, but only that some of those norms must be.) Moreover, this communication must be potentially accessible to nonparticipants, since without such accessibility the practice would cease to exist when its current participants dropped out. The communication required by a practice, then, must be linguistic. The idea of linguistic communication can be understood broadly here: a set of public signs with assignable meanings. But practices do require language.

This idea of practices as discursive is akin to Ludwig Wittgenstein's idea that language-games are central components of forms of life. Although my term *practice* can be read either as "language-game" or as "form of life" (Wittgenstein was notoriously obscure about these notions), I believe that the approach to practices that I am advocating is of a piece with Wittgenstein's own perspective.

Now some might want to object to the idea that practices require language by saying that such a requirement would preclude nonhuman animals from engaging in practices, since they don't have language. This is a sticky topic, since the question of whether, say, dolphins have a language or whether chimpanzees communicate in what we would want to call a language is an unresolved one. It depends in part on where the limits of the use of the term *language* ought to lie. Although in the next chapter of the book we'll spend some time looking at languages, what I say there will not settle the particular question of whether we should say that dolphins or chimpanzees have language. There is a related point, however, that will at least give us a running start in addressing the issue. From the discussion so far about practices, you can see that practices are created and sustained through interpersonal interaction. Some of that interaction can be nonlinguistic (how to balance on a bicycle), but some has to be linguistic (rules of the road a bicyclist should know). Whatever else practices involve, then, they must be capable of enough linguistic formulation to be able to communicate whatever norms are required in order to sustain the practice. So whether we ultimately employ the term *practices* to describe dolphin or chimpanzee (or other nonhuman animal) behavior will be linked to what kinds of capacity for linguistic communication we see in these animals. Although this observation doesn't settle the issue, it at least says something about what one would need to know in order to settle it.

At this point, we have a general sense of what a practice is. Let me turn next to a distinction that one philosopher wants to make between different kinds of practices, and then discuss in a preliminary way why practices are important to who we are. Recall that at this moment the goal is to get as good an initial grasp as we can of the idea of a practice. As the discussion unfolds, and as we look at how practices are involved in important aspects of our lives, that grasp should become more refined. But in turning over the distinction this philosopher wants to propose, we can already begin to deepen the current understanding of a practice.

In his book *Social Practices,* Theodore Schatzki distinguishes between two types of practices, which he calls "dispersed" and "integrative." Dispersed practices earn their name because they are dispersed among various integrative practices. He uses explaining, imagining, following rules, and describing as examples of dispersed practices. In the examples we have looked at so far—which are all examples of what Schatzki would call "integrative" practices—activities such as explaining and following rules would come into play. When I taught my eldest son (and later, my daughter) how to ride a bicycle, for instance, I explained how turning the handlebars to the right turns the bike to the right, and how the bike turns left with a left turn of the handlebars. My son and daughter learned how to follow the rule of riding the bike on the right side of the road. We can see dispersed practices elsewhere, too: in chess, one imagines how a position would look if one made a certain move. One also imagines in counseling others how it would feel to be the person being counseled.

Among the examples Schatzki cites under the heading of integrative practices, there are religious practices, practices of cooking, banking practices, and celebratory practices. We have also seen various sporting practices, and can add scientific practices and criminal practices to the list as well. These practices are called "integrative" because they bring together, each in a different way, the dispersed practices we have just considered. As Schatzki emphasizes, different integrative practices have their own organization of rules, of non-rule types of normativity, and of goals and emotions and bodily involvements. To see what he means by an integrative practice, let's take a brief look at an example of one: Chinese cooking. And to make it more concrete, let's stick with stir-frying.

When you stir-fry, the key is to heat the food quickly, so that it's both crisp and hot. We've all had overdone stir-fry, and—in addition to its being less nutritious than crisply done food—its texture is wilted and it doesn't taste so good either. But in order to cook the food crisply and thoroughly, one of the rules of stir-fry is to cut thin slices of vegetables and meat and to have the pan already hot when you drop in the food. And there is a way to stir the food with a spatula or wooden spoon while it is cooking, one that can't be explained very easily. The best way to learn the stirring method is to watch someone who knows how to do it, to get a sense of how to move the wrist and how to turn the slices of food in the pan.

Then there's the matter of how long to cook the food, which is also something you have to get a feel for. You can go by the rules, which dictate certain amounts of time for meat and less time for vegetables. But if you're good at stir-fry (which I'm not), then you don't need to keep your eye on the clock. You can tell when the food's done by looking at it.

Finally, there are the colors. An interesting stir-fry not only tastes good and is nutritious but has an attractive arrangement of colors, too. Cooking experience can yield a sense of which vegetables will harmonize with others. Cookbooks can also offer good suggestions. But a stir-fry with, say, only green vegetables may taste as good as it likes but will still not really satisfy since its appeal to the palate will be offset by its offense to the eye.

In this example, we can see rules (e.g., pan temperature and thin slices), non-rule normativity (e.g., color mix), goals (taste, color, nutrition), bodily movements (stirring with the spatula), and emotions (the satisfaction of a successful meal, the enjoyment of the cooking itself). We have on hand an integrative practice. And we also have what Schatzki calls "dispersed" practices. There is the describing of the appropriate pan temperature and the following of rules to achieve it, the explaining of the reasons for thin slicing, and there is even imagining with regard to the color arrangement. We could add others as well: for example, the reading of the cookbook instructions. This last dispersed practice is, granted, more important for beginners than for accomplished practitioners of stir-fry, but it provides an example of what I referred to above as the use of language in order to initiate others into a current practice.

This example does seem to give some credence to the idea that there are two types of practices, dispersed and integrative. Nevertheless, I must confess that I am not entirely comfortable with the idea. Specifically, I'm not entirely comfortable with dispersed practices being called "practices." They seem to me more like skills that are put to use in specific practices and that receive their content from the practices into which they are integrated.

The primary reason I want to reserve the term *practices* only for the integrative practices that Schatzki discusses has to do with the larger question behind the investigation of practices: the question of who we are. Of course, we are people who describe, imagine, read, follow orders, and so on. But in asking who each of us is, we really want something more fine-grained than that. Who we are is constituted not only by our ability to do these things but also by the uses to which we put these abilities, uses that are almost exclusively in the course of Schatzki's integrative practices. Some of the reasons for this will become clearer in the next part of the book, but I can cast some light upon them here. When we follow rules, for instance, we usually do so because there is an end we are trying to achieve, an end that has something to do with what others around us are doing and that is achieved by means of some kind of socially recognized norms. The same goes for describing, reading, explaining, and even imagining. (Take, for instance, the imagining of a color arrangement in stir-frying, or the imagining of an advertisement's layout by a commercial artist.)

This is not to say that we are all automatons, and that explaining and following orders are just mechanical operations that society programs into us. The goals we choose, the style with which we follow rules, and (as we'll see more in the next chapter of the book) our capacity to change and criticize practices all militate against a mechanistic view of practice-following. But the motivation for and the content of many dispersed practices occur by means of the integrative practices, and therefore the latter gives us a more keenly focused glimpse of who we are than the former. So, regarding the question of who we are, it seems best to reserve the term *practices* only for integrative practices.

There is another problem with using the word "practices" for the skills Schatzki describes. It is related to the problem we just saw, but does not have to do with any weakness in using the idea of practices to approach the question of who we are. It is that what Schatzki calls "dispersed practices" and what I am calling "abilities" or "skills" have by themselves very little or no content. By that, I mean that the substance or subject matter of most of these abilities comes from the practices within which they take place. Take describing, for example. When I describe something for someone, I don't just go about describing every aspect of that thing. My description is guided by the purposes I take my listener to have in wanting to know about the thing I'm describing, or alternatively, by my goals in offering the description.

If, for instance, I am describing for my students the famous passage in Jean-Paul Sartre's *Being and Nothingness* that analyzes the actions of a waiter, I don't talk about the typesetting of the page on which the passage occurs, or the number of times the word "waiter" appears in the passage. These things certainly *are* descriptions of the passage, and under certain conditions might be relevant. (Imagine that I wanted to reprint the passage in an edited collection of Sartre's writings, and the publisher wanted to know how long the passage was. Then facts about typesetting might be relevant in describing the passage.) I *do* talk about the waiter's smoothness, his seeming indifference to his work, his sense of playing a role that does not seem to have anything much to do with him.

Describing, then, as an ability, is something abstract that only comes to fruition in specific acts of describing, and moreover in acts that are guided by the purposes of the description. To put the point another way: the content of descriptions is determined by the purposes to which those descriptions are being put. If this is right, then integrative practices give describing its content, since the purposes to which most descriptions are put are tied up with integrative practices.

But a practice without a content seems a funny thing to call a

"practice," doesn't it? It seems more at home as a "skill" or an "ability" that is put to use in the course of various practices. This, then, is
the other reason I want to reserve the term *practices* for the integrative
practices that Schatzki describes.

So, to sum up the last few pages: because of the relation of integrative practices to the question of who we are and because of the
content-less nature of dispersed practices by themselves, it seems best
to think of practices as integrating, in specific ways, various groups of
dispersed skills such as explaining, reading, describing, imagining, and
the like.

Now someone might want to ask here if it is possible to have a skill
that falls into the category of dispersed practices, a skill that is used
somehow—but *not* integrated into a practice. Is it possible to have one
of these skills displayed on its own without its occurring within the
context of a practice? I'm not sure what to say to that. I can think of
marginal cases. For example, when imagining passes over into daydreaming, insofar as daydreaming is not a practice—and at best it lies
on the outer margins of practices, although it is certainly affected by
them—then we may have an example of a freestanding skill of the
type that Schatzki wants to call a "dispersed practice." I'm not too
worried about examples like these, though. Since I want to show how
practices are largely determinative of who we are, if the crucial aspects
of the skills I am discussing do receive their content from practices,
and if practices do turn out to be largely determinative of who we are,
then the freestanding existence of these skills on the margins of our
lives will do no harm to my argument. If I had wanted to argue that
all of who we are is a matter of practices, then I would need to show
that these skills or abilities can *only* appear in the context of practices.
But since I gave up the first goal pages ago, there seems no harm in
allowing these skills to flourish at the margins of our practices if they
so choose.

A final note before we turn to the role of practices in determining
who we are. I have taken issue with Schatzki's distinction between
dispersed and integrative practices in order to deepen our understanding of the concept of a practice. It is not, of course, unusual in
philosophical literature for philosophers to criticize positions taken by
other philosophers. Often this criticism aims to refine ideas to which

the criticizer is sympathetic. There are, of course, philosophers who make their living just trying to undermine the ideas of others—but those philosophers are almost never worth reading or hearing. They see the task of philosophy as tearing down the scaffolding others have built in order to try to see who and where we are. Like the school gossip who can't get a date, these philosophers glory in watching others fail. At philosophy conferences, I have heard it said more often than I care to recall that one philosopher, having heard another one give a paper, "cut him off at the knees." How it is that making another philosopher look foolish in front of an audience or in print is supposed to advance our understanding of ourselves has always been a mystery to me. Usually, a well-placed revision or sympathetic criticism is enough to reorient a position that has gone awry. (There is, of course, a place for sharp criticism. But much less of a place than some of my philosophical cohorts seem to believe.)

In the case of my criticism of Schatzki, what I have offered is more in the neighborhood of a friendly amendment than even a criticism. In fact, I think of Schatzki's book on practices as the best technical book I've seen on the subject. He discusses issues I can only gloss here, and his work would probably accommodate a lot of what I claim here on behalf of practices that he does not mention. For those who find the approach of this book to be persuasive, and want a more technical treatment of some of the issues I raise, there is probably no better book out there to read than Schatzki's.

WHY PRACTICES ARE IMPORTANT TO WHO WE ARE: AN INITIAL APPROACH

At this moment, we have a more or less general understanding of what practices are. I have offered a definition of them, discussed various aspects of the definition, and, in the review of Schatzki's work, tried to give a more concrete sense—although still a very broad sense—of what practices look like. The next two chapters of this book will look at several aspects of practices in detail. In Chapter 2, I'll try to show that what we think of as our knowledge is inseparable from the practices to which we are committed. Finally, in Chapter 3, I'll try to draw out the connections between our moral values and our practices, and between our political relationships and our practices. At the end of the day, I hope to have presented a fairly compelling case for the idea that who we are is largely a matter of the practices in which we are engaged.

Before turning to the next two chapters, however, I'll need to give a clearer view of what practices are. In order to do that, I will—as we say on our exams—compare and contrast practices with several other social institutions: communities, civil societies, and cultures. This comparing and contrasting should, if I do it right, both give a better idea of what practices are and help situate practices in the larger social field. But even before embarking on that task, it is probably worth pausing a moment to take an initial look at the importance of practices. After all, spending forty or fifty pages discussing an idea without any sense of what the point of that discussion is requires that I ask you to take on faith more than that to which I'm entitled. "Trust me, it really does come to something in the end" doesn't strike me as a particularly compelling claim to make when the area under discussion is philosophical in nature. So let's turn a moment, in a light and breezy way, to some of the roles practices play in determining who we are.

I'll use myself as a case study. I'm involved in a number of practices in my work, at home, and outside the home. Let's take one of each. At work, I'm a philosopher. Now being a philosopher is not merely a matter of blindly performing certain acts, no more than being a sales representative or a nurse is. Being a philosopher involves a recognition of particular rules and norms, it involves being oriented toward particular goals, and it involves being cognizant of the work of others who also call themselves philosophers. Among the goals of philosophical practice are to arrive at certain broad truths about ourselves and our world and—since most philosophers are also teachers—to introduce others to the discipline of arriving at certain broad truths about ourselves and our world. If all of this sounds kind of loose, that's because it is. One of the things philosophers argue about is the nature of philosophy itself, so I don't want to prejudice things too much one way or another concerning the goals of philosophy.

If I were to isolate one of the distinctive features of philosophical practice, however, I might pick the fact that philosophical practice is more consciously self-reflective than other practices. By this I mean that when a philosopher offers a certain perspective on something, in evaluating that perspective one always asks how well the claims that make up that perspective fit into the perspective itself. This is still a little abstract, so let me give an example. Suppose you want to claim that all truth is relative to what a given society thinks is true. In philosophical practice, it is fair game to ask whether the claim "All truth is relative to what a given society thinks is true" is itself only true relative to what our society thinks about it. In fact, that's probably one of the first questions you'll be asked. (I'll ask it myself later on in Chapter 2.) What that question does is force you back in a self-reflective way to what you've just said. Does what you've just said fit into the framework of the perspective you're trying to build? Philosophical practice often involves that form of self-reflection and relies upon it to a much greater extent than other practices do.

Conscious self-reflection is not the only characteristic of philosophical practice, but it is one. And as a philosopher, I am often engaged in it. Now my engagement in conscious self-reflection is not just a blind activity. How could it be? Moreover, I don't do it only when I'm treating philosophical texts. Conscious self-reflection has become part of who I am. It is, to put it another way, part of my personal style. And it comes to me from my engagement in philosophical practice.

Now one might want to argue here that the practice does not create this aspect of me; rather, it is because I am already consciously self-reflective that I came to philosophy in the first place. Perhaps. But even assuming that to be true, this part of me would probably wither or at least become more marginal without the reinforcement of the practice. To see how, let me use a far-fetched example. Imagine that there were a long, drawn-out civil war going on in the United States, one in which I got deeply involved. The immediacy and urgency of winning the civil war would orient me toward the tasks and ways of thinking needed to shore up the battle on my side. And conscious self-reflection is not generally counted among the primary winning tactics. (Of more use might be a reflection on what the enemy is likely to do.) The longer the war, the more who I am will be formed by the various engagements I make in helping to prosecute it; by contrast, conscious self-reflection will become less and less a part of who I am.

Here someone might want to press the point against me in another way—by recourse to genetic inheritance. Suppose that conscious self-reflection were a matter of genetic inheritance. Suppose the capacity for and inclination toward that kind of thinking were somehow programmed into people to a greater or lesser extent. *Then* wouldn't it be that something other than the practice of philosophy contributed to that aspect of who I am?

Not necessarily. Biologists seem to think that for many genetic traits there is no systematic correlation between possessing the trait and displaying it in one's behavior. Although genetic inheritance may influence things like conscious self-reflection, there is no immediate reason to believe that a genetic trait (or combination of traits) for conscious self-reflection—assuming that there is such a thing—would necessarily result in my being consciously self-reflective. This trait or traits might incline me toward conscious self-reflection, *given the right conditions*. But it may well be that there has to be something in the environment that brings that trait to the fore. What kind of something might that be? Well, in my case, the practice of philosophy would certainly fill the bill. So even if we grant genetic inheritance a role, and even an important role, in the formation of this particular aspect of who I am, nevertheless it is likely that without the proper practices in place, that aspect might still never arise.

But now an objection might come from another quarter. Bear in mind that my general point at this moment is that practices are important in determining who people are; the specific point is that the practice of philosophy is important in determining who I am, who Todd May is. Someone might want to grant me the specific point while denying me the more general one. He or she might turn to me and say, "Listen, a career in philosophy involves a special sort of practice. Most people don't have careers like that. They have jobs that mean very little to them, jobs whose purpose (as far as they are concerned) is solely to make ends meet: pay the rent, feed the kids, meet the mortgage payments. Jobs like that don't make any real contribution to who people are, even though they involve people in specific practices on a daily basis, and often for many of their waking hours."

I certainly don't want to argue that all jobs necessarily contribute in a meaningful way to who people are. That *would* be saying too much. It may well be that if people resist the influences of their jobs sufficiently, then the practices those jobs consist of may play only a marginal role in who people are. But situations like that seem to me more the exception than the rule. Most people seem fairly profoundly affected by what they do day-to-day. Let me offer a couple of for-instances. Psychologists often have a tendency to analyze people's motives psychologically even when they aren't in the office. (As a recovering psychologist myself, and one who has been in several intimate relationships with other psychologists, I can testify to this tendency firsthand.) People involved in various aspects of business often think about personal matters in terms of efficiency, and even cost-efficiency. And those who are deeply engaged in politics often think about many aspects of their lives in strategic terms, terms that suggest issues of positioning and struggle.

These examples should not be surprising. A practice (or group of practices) in which people engage for forty hours a week or so would seem likely to make a significant contribution to how they see themselves and their world and how they act in it, even during off-hours.

What's more, think of how difficult it often is to distance oneself from one's job. We've all had jobs we hated and wanted nothing to do with when we left the workplace. But jobs have a tendency to follow us around after work. Not only do we think about the job itself—the work. We also think in terms of the practice that job involves, terms that it usually takes effort and discipline to overcome.

So far, I've been discussing how work practices help contribute to who we are. Let me turn now to another area of practices: domestic practices. As a specific example, let's think about child rearing. Child rearing, even if we want to think of it as a single practice rather than several, certainly intersects with a number of practices, many of them outside the home: teaching, various sports, sometimes religious practices, and the like. As a father, my involvement with my children is (as any parent knows) something that affects who I am in important ways.

By teaching my kids, by trying to be a role model for them, by making sure I can support them financially, I experience changes in myself. Some of these changes are for the better; some are for the worse. On the better side, having kids often helps you to see the world from other angles. By having to look at the world through your children's eyes, you come to realize that your way of seeing things is not the only way in which the world can be viewed. (This is something that can happen in a marriage, too, but since the partners in a marriage frequently are more nearly peers, the difference in viewpoint is often less radical.) On the down side, the sense of responsibility that parenthood grants can undermine one's willingness to take interesting chances with one's life. Parenthood tends to push one toward conformity and away from creativity.

Is child rearing—which clearly has much to do with who a parent is—really a practice (or group of practices), though? It is. First, it is goal-directed. The aim of child rearing is to produce an adult who can make his or her way through the world. Different parents, of course, emphasize different skills or personal characteristics in trying to achieve this aim. For some, self-discipline is the most important thing, while for others it may be a sense of security or confidence, and for still others, intellectual or athletic achievement (or some combination of these). But in the end, if parents are engaged in the practice of child rearing, the goal of that engagement will be some form of autonomous adulthood.

Now by saying that child rearing has a goal, I don't intend to demean the here-and-now enjoyment of the practice. I can imagine parents reading the last paragraph and thinking: Wait a minute! Child rearing isn't some sort of parental regimen that takes its pleasure only from achieving a certain goal. There is a pleasure, even an erotics, of child rearing that brings many moments of joy that aren't subsumed into the aim of providing for adulthood. True enough. When I say that practices are goal-directed, I don't want to be understood as saying that all the joys of the practice lie in the achieving of the goal. While having a goal is structurally necessary in order for there to be a practice (with the possible marginal exceptions, like sitting Zen, that I noted earlier), that does not imply that the only point of engaging in a practice is to achieve its goal.

To see why, let me spend a moment on another group of practices: sports. Most sports fit the definition of practices pretty cleanly. And the goal of many sports is to prevail in certain kinds of competitions. But that isn't all there is to the enjoyment of participation in sports. The feeling of being in shape, the sensual pleasure of straining against one's own bodily limits, the knowledge that one looks good to those to whom one would like to be physically attractive—all of these aspects of sports also play into the enjoyment of participating in sporting practices.

So it is with child rearing. While producing an adult who can successfully navigate the world is the goal of child rearing, there are many pleasures to be taken along the way. (And in fact, it may well be that a parent who is incapable of taking any of those pleasures may be less likely to achieve the goal of producing an autonomous adult. But that's another story.) But if child rearing is goal-directed, does it also have the other components of a practice—socially governed norms and regularities of behavior? The regularities, of course, are there: playing with kids, disciplining them, helping them with their homework. Parenthood may have its creative aspects, but does tend toward a certain kind of regularization. That's one of the aspects of the conformity I mentioned earlier toward which parenthood leans.

As far as norms go, parenthood is directed by sets of changing—and sometimes conflicting—norms. (The fact of conflicting norms, as we will see when we discuss morality, does not rule out the possibility of a practice's being able to operate. It does, though, create some difficulties.) There are norms, for instance, regarding discipline, which are different from disciplinary norms from earlier generations. When I grew up, spanking was considered to be an okay form of discipline, since obedience was an overriding short-term goal of child rearing. But now that the discouragement of violence and humiliation is thought to be more significant than it used to be, spanking, with rare exceptions, is out. Talking to children about the effects of their behavior and using punishments like time-out are in. (This change seems to me all to the good, not only because the values now emphasized seem superior to obedience but also because—as a kid who always found himself in trouble—I went through large stretches of my childhood blushing beneath my pants.)

Other norms are more conflicted, such as the norms having to do with the feeding regimen of infants. Breast-feeding is considered much more important to a child's development than it was a generation ago. In fact, the willingness of some parents to frown upon those who bottle-feed, as though bottle-feeding were a form of child abuse, is often stunning to me. And yet, breast-feeding undercuts another important current norm of child raising: involvement of the father at the earliest stages of a child's development. It's not that breast-feeding and paternal involvement are incompatible. But, since feeding is a key part of an infant's relations to those around him or her, breast-feeding, while having clear nutritional merits and allowing for an early mother-child bond to develop, does create some difficulties for paternal engagement in the first months of a child's life.

These examples, and others that are probably leaping to the minds of those among you who are parents, show the norm-driven nature of child rearing. And, of course, there is a deep relationship between the three elements of the practice—the goal, the regularities, and the norms—and, moreover, a deep relationship between those three elements and who one becomes when one becomes a parent. For instance, the *goal* of adult autonomy seems to necessitate the *norm* of providing a secure environment for a child; that norm dictates (at least in our society) the necessity of at least a minimal level of financial well-being; that necessity results in *regularities* in lifestyle and narrowing of personal horizons, which also induce personal conformity—all of these are related moments in the practice of child rearing. (This, of course, is a negative example. There are plenty of positive ones. I use this example because the relationship between goal, norms, and regularities and who one is is straightforward.)

So far, we've taken a look at how engagements in a career practice and in a domestic practice can affect who one is. In order to round out this brief sketch, let me turn finally to a practice outside the home that is not career-related. For some people, such practices include sports, church, various hobbies, and so on. The practice I will discuss centers on my participation in progressive political struggle. I use it largely because it is a practice—or really, a group of practices—in which I don't participate much now, because where I live does not provide a culture for progressive change. But, having had these struggles as a central part of my life for some seven or eight years, I have been significantly formed by my participation in them. So I want to use the example of political struggle to sketch both how who I am now is partly a matter of the practices I engaged in before now, and how my no longer being engaged in those practices—at least very deeply—also affects who I am now.

From around 1985 through 1992, I volunteered much of my time for a variety of progressive causes. Among the struggles I was most involved in were those for divestment from South Africa and for the political rights of Palestinians. But I also had a hand in actions against aid to the contras and against racism, as well as in pro-choice, anti-military, and union struggles. In several of these struggles—in good part because I had time to contribute—I assumed a leadership role. A leadership role in grassroots political campaigns is a lot like leadership roles in military engagements (or so my military friends tell me). One is constantly thinking in terms of strategies and tactics: taking account of the possible moves the other side will make, maneuvering in ways that are difficult to counter, trying to win the sympathy of the media and the public, doing both short-term and long-term planning, dealing with splits and factions within one's own side—and, ultimately, seeing oneself as playing a role in a struggle that is larger than oneself.

Let me flesh that last characteristic out a bit. There is a tendency for people who find themselves at a comfortable standard of living to have difficulty seeing very far past the limits of their immediate world. Who's bickering with whom at work, how the kids are doing at school, the current state of our marriages, whether there will be enough money to take interesting vacations this year, who might be free for a beer on Thursday night: this is the stuff that fills much of our reflective space. What usually alters this pedestrian way of living is a crisis. During crisis moments, we tend to pull back from our immediate engagements and look at ourselves within a broader framework. At these times we see the threads that bind us to a larger world, and ask ourselves which threads are meaningful to us and which we should let go.

Political struggles can be a lot like the personal crises that compel one to widen one's perspective on the world. It's hard to worry too terribly that the pay raise you got was smaller than it might be when you also know that half a world away there are people who are forcing parents to watch their kids starve. Participating in a larger struggle helps you see your immediate concerns in the wider context within which they arise. At least that's what it did for me and for many of the people with whom I worked.

This kind of outlook affected who I was, and in some ways it still affects me. It affected me not only in what I did but also in *how* I did it. Gaining a sense of the wider perspective within which my own life unfolded not only led me to do things I would not otherwise have done—like engage in political organizing—but also introduced me to a way of seeing things that changed how I looked upon the non-political parts of my life. It would be hard to describe exactly how I was affected. Certain experiences lend a coloration to one's life that's hard to put into words. Let me say only that a calm sense of purpose often reigned where I might previously have been anxious and casting about. This doesn't exactly capture what was different, but it is often difficult to capture subtle alterations in the emotional textures of one's life. I hope it at least gives a feel for what the difference was—and is. (I am hesitant to call it a change in what is "inside" me as opposed to what is "outside," since the idea of practices should lead us away from thinking that there is a strict division between inside and outside.)

Now I am several years away from the height of my political involvement. Is this way of seeing things still with me? In some sense yes, and in some sense no. I still strive to view myself in the larger context of the world's situation; I think about where I am in relation to where others on the planet find themselves; I remain sensitive to the oppression around me and how it makes the lives of others more difficult than mine is. So the engagement in a past practice has continued to inform who I am. By the same token, the central importance of those changes has worn away somewhat. It is easier for me to forget my place in the world generally and focus too much upon my own personal concerns, frustrations, and accomplishments. Sometimes I find myself working to remind myself of lessons that I once lived more viscerally, lessons that were more naturally a part of who I was.

From this I draw the twofold conclusion that first, who one is is partly a matter of the practices one has engaged in previously, and second, current practices have a tendency to pull one's "self"—who one is—away from past practices, particularly from past practices that are very different from current ones.

In discussing the examples of my career, my family, and my political work, I have tried to give an initial sense of how participation in practices shapes who one is. I don't think I've said anything very controversial or anything very deep. So much the better. It seems to me that we—we people, and especially we philosophers—tend to miss a lot of what we might see by moving too quickly away from the surface of things. We want to find some underlying principle that explains everything that lies in front of us, and as a result, we stop looking at what's in front of us, missing the lessons that such observation might teach.

This is not to deny that we have reason to go below the surface. In the following chapters of the book, I will move from the surface of practices to their underlying structures. But there is more to be gained (more than we are often tempted to think) by sticking with what's in front of us, as the philosophers who are called phenomenologists have taught. And that surely seems to be the case with regard to practices. We need to look more steadily at what we do every day. In asking ourselves who we are, we have ignored the practices that make up so much of our lives, in part because they are right there in front of us, seeming to require no particular thought. So we pass them by, looking for something deeper to explain us to ourselves.

This looking beyond practices has led us to two specific kinds of errors or illusions that we frequently fall into when asking ourselves the question of who we are. These two illusions are worth pausing over, because they will allow us to deepen the question of who we are by bringing it along paths that people think about when they think nobody else is noticing. Following a hallowed philosophical tradition, I'll christen these errors. I'll call the first kind of error *the illusion of the secret self,* and the second, *the illusion of metaphysical depth.* And, since looking at these illusions will take us in some new directions in asking the question of who we are, I'll introduce a section break.

TWO ILLUSIONS: THE SECRET SELF
AND METAPHYSICAL DEPTH

The illusion of the secret self is one I see all the time with beginning philosophy students, and still, after years of philosophical study, find myself lured into from time to time. Under the sway of the illusion of the secret self, we try to discover who we are by abstracting away all of the outside influences that affect us, all of the social regularities in which we participate, all of our day-to-day engagements, in order to find the "real me" that lies beneath it all. The question "Who am I, really?" is approached by hacking away at the entirety of our participation in the world and calling what is left over the answer. The hope is that there *is* something left over (after subtracting all one's social engagements and public behavior) that is unique and special, the key to who we really are.

We all know the temptation of this illusion. It's difficult *not* to be tempted by it, particularly in an advanced technological society. We live in a world in which we are plugged into social roles of one kind or another—often impersonal ones—and periodically we feel the pull of these roles toward some kind of blind conformity that seems to be a betrayal of who we feel ourselves to be. We experience alienation, and comfort ourselves by reflecting that we aren't really what our co-workers, friends, or family think we are. We are something different, something apart from all that. If we were just a bunch of different social roles, then what makes us either unique or irreplaceable? After all, social roles can (at least in principle) be played by many different people, as I argued above when discussing the impossibility of a completely private practice. If that's true, then what makes me *me*, as opposed to somebody else, can't be the social role or roles that I play. It must be something left over after those social roles are exhausted, something uniquely my own that, if it makes its appearance at all, does not do so *through* the social roles that I play but *in spite of them*. Therefore, if there is a me at all that answers to the question "Who am I?" it must lie in a secret self, underneath or outside of my social—or at least socially regulated—behavior.

In addressing the worries that give rise to the illusion of the secret self, we need to concede right off that practices do entail roles that are socially normatively constrained, that is to say, roles that are given by social rules and other norms that limit and guide what we can do if we are to remain participants in that practice. (As we will see later, these are rules and norms that can be changed, but only in exchange for other rules and norms.) This, however, does not seem to me to be a bad thing as far as who one is goes. In fact, it seems to be a necessary condition of being anything at all in the world. It is largely because of, not in spite of, the social roles we play in our practices that we are who we are. Without social roles to play in practices, we would all be like those kids running aimlessly around the playground that I mentioned in the discussion of what is and what is not a practice. I suppose that such aimless running around is being *something,* but if that's all there is of us it isn't much of anything, and certainly not the kind of thing calculated to provide a rich sense of self.

Think of someone like Mickey Mantle, or Nelson Mandela, or Virginia Woolf. Is what makes Mickey Mantle who he was something apart from his participation in baseball? Is Nelson Mandela truly Mandela—the real thing—apart from his role in South African political life? Should we say of Virginia Woolf that who she really was was something apart from her role as a writer? Obviously not, in all cases. What made these people who they were (and are) was not something apart from the roles they played in the practices for which we know them; rather, it was the way in which they played their roles. Without having played those roles, they would not have been who they were but would have been other people entirely. (Not people with different names—same names, different people.) And had they no role to play in any practice at all, whom would they have been? Perhaps just people running aimlessly around a playground. (Which is really hard to envision in Virginia Woolf's case.) In order for one to have an answer to the question "Who am I?" one needs to talk about the practices in which one is engaged.

Now here someone may want to stop me and say that I've performed a sleight of hand. Mickey Mantle, one might argue, was who he was not simply because of his being a baseball player but because of the *way* in which he played baseball. What I've done is mix up two things that are separate, that the idea of the secret self would recognize as separate. The first is the role someone plays, which is social and which lots of people can fulfill. The second is the way in which someone plays the role, a mode that is individual and that originates in the secret self, defining who one really is. If that is right, then the secret self is not an illusion, but the real answer to the question of who one is. And it is an answer that has nothing to do with practices, since it is separate from the roles those practices involve.

This line of thinking is seductive, but it doesn't work. You can't separate the role one plays from the way in which one plays it. With Mickey Mantle, there aren't two things going on, a baseball player and a way of being a baseball player. There's only one thing: a way of being a baseball player. Nelson Mandela had a way of playing his role—actually, his various roles—in the political struggle for a democratic South Africa. And the magisterial way he had of playing those roles, a magisterial manner that he continued to demonstrate throughout his presidency, was not separate from the roles themselves: it was precisely a way of being those roles, of being in those practices. Ditto for Virginia Woolf. Her way of being a writer was precisely a way of *being a writer.* It was the "how" of engaging in a social role in a recognizable practice.

Looking at things in this way allows us to see how it is possible to be defined in who one is by one's practices without one's having to lose any of the uniqueness that the illusion of the secret self wants to protect. People's uniqueness, inasmuch as they possess any, is often given in the ways in which they participate in their practices. Indeed, the descriptions of their uniqueness are often descriptions of the ways in which they participate in or contribute to those practices. Mickey Mantle's uniqueness lay in being a certain kind of baseball player, as did Virginia Woolf's uniqueness in being a certain kind of writer and Nelson Mandela's in being a certain kind of political resister and statesman. (Each of these people may have been unique in other ways as well, but for simplicity's sake I am sticking with a limited range of their engagements.)

This way of seeing things also helps us explain a less discussed phenomenon as well: lack of uniqueness. We have just considered several people who are unique in what they do (or did). But many of us aren't so unique. We play our various social roles, participating in our practices without bringing anything terribly new to bear upon those practices. We are more or less anonymous in that sense. This is especially true insofar as we come to identify in a blind way with our roles in those practices, participating in them without thinking about what the point of that participation is. What the illusion of the secret self tries to do is to save us from anonymity by saying that our uniqueness lies elsewhere than in our participation in practices. It lies, instead, in a secret self that everyone has, apart from what we happen to do in the practices in which we are engaged.

This seems to me to be a cop-out. The fact is that many of us aren't terribly unique, even though we would like to be. Moreover, if we really want to achieve some kind of uniqueness, what it requires is creative work, not a way of seeing things that makes us turn out to have been unique all along. We may have our little quirks and corners of eccentricity, but those margins of uniqueness neither lend us any particular nobility nor say very much about who we are. For most of us, our lives are largely caught up in practices that define us without our redefining them.

Failing to redefine the character of the practices in which we are engaged doesn't mean that we have no personal significance. We may gain a sense of significance by our contributions to the ongoing existence of the practice—and if the practice is any good, then we should. But for most of us it would be thinking too highly of ourselves for us to affirm any deep measure of our uniqueness. Our personal significance, the illusion of the secret self notwithstanding, often lies in our contributions to matters that are larger than we are rather than in the uniqueness of the contributions themselves.

This is not to say that those of us who aren't unique in our participation in various practices aren't unique at all. There may be aspects of our behavior—what I called, above, "quirks and eccentricities"— that distinguish us from others who may be engaged in much the same practices. That type of uniqueness, however, is usually more marginal than the uniqueness of a Mickey Mantle or a Nelson Mandela or a Virginia Woolf, and in two senses. First, unlike the decidedly unique contributions to various practices, personal quirks and eccentricities rarely have an effect on the way others (or very many others) live their lives. Nelson Mandela, to take the obvious example, has had a deep effect on the lives of millions, an effect that cannot be compared to a personal quirk or eccentricity. Second, these quirks and eccentricities often are not deeply characteristic of who we are. I, for instance, am more deeply a philosopher and a father than a guy who says "Yo" to colleagues at a southern university, although I have been told that the latter is considered a signature quirk of mine.

Now here again, someone might want to raise an objection. This one is a little more pointed than the objection that one can distinguish the practices people are engaged in from the way in which they are engaged in them, but is still related to it. Bear in mind that the larger issue motivating all of this discussion is whether our practices define who we are in a deep way. The new objection runs something like this: Okay, there is no distinction between the way in which a person participates in a particular practice and the participation itself. Nevertheless, people have personal styles that characterize the ways in which they participate in the different practices across their lives. Although the practices may be different, the styles may be the same. And wouldn't personal uniqueness—and who one is—lie in the style itself rather than in the various participations in different practices?

An example would probably help to illuminate the force of this objection. I have a friend who, no matter what practice he engages in, does so with a sort of self-effacing irony that is at once charming and hysterically funny. He's a magazine editor, and such irony often seems to be a barrier against madness in that profession. He's also a runner, and his irony contrasts with the typical funereal solemnity of serious runners. In his friendships and love relationships, he also carries himself in this self-effacing, ironic way. Wouldn't we want to say of my friend that who he is is this particular style or way of being rather than the practices upon which he brings this style to bear? And if so, then wouldn't we say that who he is is a matter of something outside of his practices—if not exactly a secret self, then a personal style?

I am sympathetic to this objection. There is certainly something right in saying that who a person is depends at least in part on the style of behavior they bring to their activities. Moreover, the idea of style is not reducible to the mere *fact* of participation in practices, since it is a *way* of participating in practices. In that sense, style is something about a person that answers to the question of who he or she is without being solely a matter of practices. But in another sense, style *is* tied up with practices—even a personal style that someone exhibits across practices. The reason for this is that personal style is usually displayed as a way of being *in* one's various practices. Just as Mickey Mantle was not a way of being a baseball player as distinct from just being a baseball player, so my friend's self-effacing irony is not some quality that's added onto his participation in various practices: it's his way of participating in those practices. Personal style is not some secret characteristic that one possesses and then attaches to one's behavior, as though it were stored deep in someone's personality and then pulled out and mixed with the behavior itself. It is a way of behaving. Style and behavior are inseparable. And if that's true, then style and participation in practices—the latter, after all, is a matter of behavior—are equally inseparable.

The upshot of this line of thinking, then, is that while the objection I have raised against myself—that who one is is partly a matter of one's style, and that style is not reducible simply to the fact of participating in practices—is right, personal style is not something completely separable from one's practices either. To put the point a different way: personal style, although a defining characteristic of who one is, is not some kind of a secret self but rather a way of being a non-secret, or public, self. What this gives us is another avenue for personal uniqueness that recognizes the importance of practices without succumbing to the anonymity that playing one's role in practices might seem to imply.

Before turning to the second illusion that prevents us from seeing the importance of practices in answering the question of who we are, let me point in passing to another way in which one can display uniqueness while still being largely a participant in practices. So far, in addressing the question of personal uniqueness, I have denied the plausibility of the idea of a secret self as a way to answer the question of who we are, but I have conceded the relevance of personal style. There is another path to uniqueness as well, one that runs directly through practices.

Sometimes personal uniqueness can occur in the *combination* of practices in which one chooses to participate. We all know people who participate in practices that surprise us, given the other practices in which they're involved. Whether they're bankers who write poetry or priests who play jazz or academics who lift weights, people can combine practices that, for one reason or another (often blind tradition), aren't usually merged in the same person. This combination of seemingly disparate practices can lend someone at least two types of personal uniqueness. First, those who participate in disparate practices may be unique just in the fact of combining those practices. Since who one is is deeply tied to one's practices, and since we have here a unique combination of practices, we seem to have uncovered a form of personal uniqueness.

The other, more interesting way in which participating in disparate practices can lend a certain uniqueness to a person occurs through a sort of cross-fertilization. Disparate practices often require very different skills and different ways of looking at things. The skills and outlooks associated with banking, for instance, don't readily combine with those associated with poetry. (For this reason, bankers and poets tend not to socialize in the same crowds. Of course, there are other reasons as well.) However, the fact that there isn't a ready overlapping of different skills and outlooks doesn't mean that there *can't* be any. Such combinations can bring out new aspects or possibilities in practices that might have been missed by those who aren't as far-flung in their involvements.

A quick example would help make this point. There is a wonderful little novel about jazz by Geoff Dyer called *But Beautiful*. It characterizes major jazz figures like Thelonious Monk and Duke Ellington, but it lies somewhere between biography and fiction. As you read the book, you become aware that its style, and the particular sliding it makes between biography and fiction, turns out to be done in a jazz mode. It's as though Dyer takes the biography as the main tune—the *head*, in jazz terms—and then weaves his own literary solos from it. Like all musicians, he comes back to the head periodically before going off again. But there is a distinct head-and-solo structure to the various chapters of the book. Now that's a case in which the influence of musical practice on literary practice brings out hidden possibilities that one might not have seen without being immersed in jazz.

I have spilled a lot of toner here discussing the issue of personal uniqueness. Before turning to the second illusion I want to scruti-

nize—the illusion of metaphysical depth—let me say a bit about why
the issue of personal uniqueness seems to rate so much attention. It
has to do with the kinds of worries that motivate the illusion of the
secret self. When we ask ourselves the question of who we are, there
are at least two ways in which we may ask it. We may word it as a
collective question: "Who are we?" Alternatively, we may word it as
an individual question: "Who am I?" Now this book asks the first
question, the question of who we are, and tries to answer it in a way
that leaves open a wide range of possible responses to the second,
more individual, question. But in asking the first question, we are
often motivated by the second one. Each of us wants to know who
we are (at least in part) in order to know who each of us is. Fair
enough. But asking the question of who I am is often motivated by
two other underlying questions: "What, if anything, makes me *me* as
opposed to someone (or just anyone) else? And what, if anything, is
significant about me?"

These can be two of the most troubling philosophical questions
we ask ourselves. If we come to think that the answer to the first
question, which is of course the question of personal uniqueness, is
"Nothing," then we begin to feel like carbon copies. We feel that
others can supplant us, and that there is no particular point to our
being in the lives we are in—as opposed to other people's inhabiting
them. (Think for a moment about the various anxieties that have
arisen recently over the possibility of human cloning and how closely
those anxieties are related to worries about personal uniqueness.)
Now, it is possible to answer the second question, about significance,
positively while the answer to the first question remains "Nothing." It
is still possible to think of our lives as having some significance without our having personal uniqueness. We make our contributions to
the world; our lives matter in some way or another, even though we
are not unique. But even if we do have some personal significance,
the sense persists that our contributions to the world could have been
made by a number of other people, even though (in each case) I
happen to make them. We may feel significant but still believe that
significance does not attach itself to us—or, for each of us, to *me*—in
the way we would hope. Instead, it somehow attaches to me acciden-
tally, not necessarily. I make the contributions that are associated with

me, to be sure, but somebody else could just as well have made them. It is simply a matter of existential chance that I happen to be in this role at this time, rather than someone else.

It is this kind of worry, I think, to which the illusion of the secret self responds. The illusion offers a sense of self that is personally unique, because it makes the answer to the question of who I am always something inside of *me*. And by calling attention to the illusory nature of the secret self, I have, in some ways, returned us to the worries that motivated it in the first place. Of course I haven't argued that everyone is the same or that there is no such thing as personal uniqueness. But I haven't guaranteed anyone personal uniqueness either. Instead, I have made personal uniqueness depend (in part) on the practices in which one engages and on the ways in which one engages in those practices. To the question of whether who one is is personally unique, then, I come down with a resounding "Maybe. That depends." It isn't as comforting as having a secret self, but it allows what seems to me the proper amount of space for the development of personal uniqueness, the only amount we can claim without fooling ourselves about who we are.

Let's turn now to the second illusion, the illusion of metaphysical depth. Recall that both illusions keep us from recognizing the importance of practices in making us who we are; they do so by forcing our attention away from our daily social engagement with the world. The illusion of the secret self does so by withdrawing from this daily social engagement into a world of private selves. The illusion of metaphysical depth does so by going beneath or beyond the self, as it were, in order to find some grounding that transcends the self and that forms the basis for what it is.

To get an initial glimpse of the illusion of metaphysical depth, think of the relation of a software programmer to his or her program. Here, the "self" of the program, the program's "what it is," doesn't come from the program itself—and certainly not from any engagement in practices—but is installed into the program by the programmer. We wouldn't want to say, except in some metaphorical sense, that the program is the self of the programmer. (And even then, a metaphor like that doesn't say anything too complimentary about the programmer.) What I think we want to say here is that the "what it is" of the program is given by the programmer, who is a force standing outside the program and acting as its "ground." After all, when something goes wrong with the program, we don't complain to the program; we go to the programmer and ask him or her to fix it.

The illusion of metaphysical depth works the same way, except that you can't ask anybody to fix anything. The idea is that who we are is not something that arises by means of our engagement with the world, but is given by some transcendent (i.e., beyond the world) character that grounds us from the outside. I call this illusion the illusion of "metaphysical depth" because we often think of the term *metaphysical* in an everyday way as referring to something beyond or beneath the physical. (In academic philosophical circles, "metaphysical" has several meanings—some of them loaded—but we can retain this everyday sense of the word for our own purposes here.)

At this point, you will undoubtedly have already recognized the prime candidate for metaphysical ground: God. Many people want to say that who we are is not a matter (or is not significantly a matter) of our practices or our engagement in the world generally, but instead a matter of some transcendental grounding; they argue that who we are is a human essence given by God and realized by us all in our mortal lives. Now depending on which God we're discussing here, that essence can be more or less fine-grained, that is to say, more or less constraining for who we are. In the Judeo-Christian tradition, however much the essence of human being is seen as derived from God, there usually remains at least some measure of free will for one to develop oneself. (Calvinism would be an exception here.) But even with free will, it is nevertheless the case that God gives us our human essence—God founds who we are in the deepest sense.

Although God is the primary candidate for a metaphysical grounding of who we are, there can be others. For some, perhaps including the philosopher Martin Heidegger, Being would be a worthy competitor. Philosophers like Immanuel Kant and Edmund Husserl were drawn to the idea of a transcendental consciousness that reflected the deepest part of who we are. In all cases, though, the same idea appears: who we are is a product of something outside our involvement in the world.

Before responding to the illusion of metaphysical depth, let me linger for a moment over a recent proposal for something that might look like a candidate for a transcendent ground, but isn't: genetic determinism. I referred to this idea earlier on, and want to come back to it now, since it resembles, in some ways, the idea of God or Being or transcendental consciousness as grounding who we are. (It perhaps has the most obvious affinities with God.) *Genetic determinism,* at least in the sphere we're discussing, is the idea that who we are is predetermined by our genetic makeup. Now, as I've already said, that claim, baldly stated, is probably false. But suppose we soften it a bit just as I softened my own claim about practices. Suppose we said that who we are is *largely* a matter of our genetic makeup. As a scientific matter, we simply don't know yet how true that claim is. However, laying aside for a moment the question of whether it's true, would we want to categorize that softened form of genetic determinism under the rubric of the illusion of metaphysical depth? After all, aren't our genes in some sense a force outside of us that determines in large part who we are, that grounds us in much the same way that a programmer grounds his or her program?

I think the answer here is *no.* There is a crucial difference between the softened form of genetic determinism (since it isn't really a determinism, let's call it "genetic influence") and the candidates for metaphysical depth. Genetic influence is a thing of this world. Our genetic influences interact with our various environmental influences, including our practices, in helping to shape who we are. Genetic influences are part of this world, and inasmuch as we can't read off who we are by reading off a printout of genetic information, we must see genetic influence as one factor in the rough-and-tumble creation of who each of us is.

This is not the case with the candidates for metaphysical depth. Since they are not of this world, but outside it—that's what makes them metaphysical—they are not caught up in the various trends and forces and interactions that make up the world. God or Being or transcendental consciousness does not interact with the world and its various components in determining who we are. The grounding element for who we are comes from beyond or beneath or above, but in any case outside the world. It would thus be a mistake to throw genetic influence in as a candidate for the illusion of metaphysical depth.

Now that we have a handle on metaphysical depth as a determinant of who we are, why do I want to call it an illusion? In an important sense, I can't make the same kind of argument for metaphysical depth being an illusion as the one I made for the secret self. In the case of the secret self, I argued that it was implausible to think that the self that is supposed to be secret is something that can be an important component of who we really are. Take Mickey Mantle out of baseball and all his other practices and do you still have Mickey Mantle any more? Do we want to say that we have a secret Mickey Mantle that is the real Mickey Mantle? Seemingly not. Of course, I could bring up some of the same considerations against the illusion of metaphysical depth, but those considerations can be met by an argument that makes things a bit more complex. Here it goes.

Suppose that I argue that some form of metaphysical depth, say God, can't be the determinant for who Mickey Mantle is, because we can't think of Mickey Mantle as being who he was outside the practice of (among other things) baseball. Moreover—and this is also a question I raised earlier—how can we think of anybody's being *anything* outside of the context of practices and their norms, the context in which a person acts? This may be fine as far as it goes—and it does go pretty far—but a reply is still available to the proponent of metaphysical depth, one not available to the proponent of the secret self. The advocate of metaphysical depth can say this: "Look, Mickey Mantle expressed who he was in his practices, but his essence came from somewhere else. The essence of Mickey Mantle either (for certain God-proponents or Being-proponents) was given by God/Being and only displayed in his practices, or (for transcendental consciousness-proponents or certain other types of God-proponents) lies in his transcendental consciousness/eternal soul, of which his particular practices are only a passing manifestation."

These two replies are going to make things a little more difficult for me. The first reply concedes everything I've said about practices, but then says that there is something that lies behind those practices and makes each participant in them what he or she really is. Sure, Mickey Mantle is given as Mickey Mantle in some sense in the practice of baseball. But that doesn't tell you who he is. That just *expresses* or *displays* who he is, in the same way that the running of a computer program just expresses or displays that program, but isn't the program itself. Who Mickey Mantle is is given by the God/Being who makes him act—or allows him to act—the way he does in particular practices. Who he is, then, to hold to the analogy, is given by a programmer—or, in keeping with tradition, a Programmer. The practices are just like the running of the program. The practices may be interesting, and they may offer us a clue as to who Mickey Mantle is, but his participation in them is not the real person. The real Mickey Mantle lies behind the practices.

The second reply takes a different approach. Like the illusion of the secret self, it moves outside practices altogether. It says that what makes a person who he or she is is not a matter of that person's practices, but of something that lies completely outside of those practices. Unlike the secret self, however, that thing that lies outside a person's practices also lies outside of that person's worldly existence. For the illusion of the secret self, the self is something that's left when all social engagements and practices are stripped away. For the second type of metaphysical depth, however, what remains is something that is left when *all of me*—as an empirical being who exists in this world both privately in my mind and publicly in my actions—when all of that is stripped away.

Although they are distinct, both of these replies on behalf of metaphysical depth share the idea that what is given in the world as we know it is not all there is, and that we have to move to a realm outside of that world in order to grasp all there is—and specifically, what it is that makes us who we are. That, of course, is the metaphysical part. But now we can see what makes these replies so difficult to counter. The illusion of metaphysical depth requires a faith in something outside the world as we know it through the sciences and related disciplines. It requires that we just accept some form of transcendent take on the world, arguing from there against the idea that who we are is largely a matter of our practices. And just as it is difficult to offer an argument *for* most of these kinds of articles of faith, so it is difficult to offer an argument *against* them. I might ask someone, "How do you know that there is a God and that that God gives each of us the foundation for who we are?" He or she might well turn around to ask me how I know that there isn't a God or (if there is) that that God doesn't give each of us the foundation for who we are.

You can see where that's going to lead.

So, in calling the illusion of metaphysical depth an "illusion," I've got to admit that I have no knockdown argument against it. I'll have to content myself with the claim that metaphysical depth just isn't something we *need* in order to give a good account of who we are. We can give a reasonable and compelling account of who we are without having to bank on articles of metaphysical faith. How can we do that? Well, it's already been done, at least in part. We have on hand a sketch of how our engagement in practices says a lot about who we are, and none of that has required any metaphysical depth. In the next two chapters of the book, I hope to fill in that sketch. In the end, where that will leave us is in the position of having an alternative that doesn't require the kind of faith that metaphysical depth requires in order to give an account of who we are. It will not allow us to claim to have vanquished all competing alternatives by showing how they just can't work. For those to whom the commitment to metaphysical depth remains important in thinking about who they are, I can say only that if such an account neglects my practices, then I'm not likely to recognize myself in it; if it does give room to practices, then I begin to be unsure why it is still needed. That doesn't prove that metaphysical depth is wrong, but it does begin to sap some of the motivation for it.

There will, of course, still be others who say that using contemporary science and related fields of knowledge (rather than metaphysics) as a background is itself a form of faith, no different from the kind of metaphysical faith that I am rejecting as an account of who we are. This is a fairly common position. It unites such diverse groups as Christian fundamentalists and certain (although by no means all) multiculturalists. The idea here is that the foundations of science, like the foundations of religion, require that we accept certain claims as true in order to get research off the ground. If that's right, then science is just another faith, like religion, and it would be just as plausible to say that we can give an account of who we are without needing science as it would be to say that we can give an account of who we are without needing religious or metaphysical depth.

I am certainly prepared to admit that there is some sort of faith involved in committing to contemporary science and related fields of knowledge over and against knowledge that is religiously grounded, and the next chapter of this book should make clear exactly what kind of faith that is. On the other hand, I'm not nearly so prepared to grant that that kind of faith is no different from metaphysical faith; for exactly the same reasons, I'm not prepared to grant that the scientific method is just as good or as bad an approach to knowledge as papal authority or the Talmud are. What science has brought us by way of *empirical knowledge* (which should be distinguished from such things as a sense of meaningfulness in our lives or a grip on our moral bearings) is an impressive set of theories that are not only consistent within themselves but also across fields. Moreover, these theories explain large parts of our world without having to rely on one mystery or another at the central point of explanation. Because of this, I think that an account of who we are that is consistent with science— although not necessarily a form *of* science, which is something very different—is better to have on hand than an account of who we are that conflicts with scientific thought. Seeing ourselves in terms of practices is in keeping with the nonmetaphysical spirit of science, and for that reason it seems to me a better account than the competing ones that require the ascent to metaphysical heights.

(Let me hasten to add that the scientific method does not seem to me to be *all* there is to knowledge—a point that will also become clearer in the next chapter. My only point here is that in situations of direct competition or conflict between science and traditional religious authority, I think we're better off with science.)

Perhaps this is a good time to sum up the last couple of sections, and then to turn and compare the idea of practices to the related ideas of community, civil society, and culture. I have been trying to motivate my claim that practices are largely constitutive of who we are— or, to put it another way, that who we are is significantly, and perhaps centrally (although not exhaustively), a matter of our practices. I did this by showing in my own case how who I am is largely a matter of the practices in which I am currently engaged and at least one practice in which I have been engaged. I moved from there to a discussion of two illusions that have prevented us from seeing the importance of practices in determining who we are. These illusions turn us away from our practices toward places that are disengaged from the world. The first illusion looks inside us, rather than in our involvement in the world; the second illusion looks beneath or beyond the world altogether. In discussing these illusions I tried to make the case for why or in what senses they were illusory, as well as to seek the motivation for each and to recognize—at least in the case of the secret self—an important truth about us that can be arrived at by looking a little more deeply into the matter: the truth about how personal style is also an important part of who we are.

PRACTICES, COMMUNITIES, CIVIL SOCIETY, CULTURE

At this point, we have on the table at least a general idea of what practices are and why they are important. From here, the discussion could go in either of two directions. On the one hand, we could look more deeply into the nature of practices, analyzing their structure and considering how our participation in them and their influences on us make us who we are. Alternatively, we could look outward, away from the internal structure of practices, to see how practices are like and unlike other related social concepts that we use to describe our social life.

In fact, we'll do both.

In the next two chapters of the book, we'll look inward, trying to show how our knowledge and our moral and political lives are largely a matter of our practices. This will entail scrutinizing the bond between aspects of our knowledge, moral commitments, and interpersonal relationships along with the internal structure of our practices. Such scrutiny should help us achieve the kind of depth of understanding that any philosophical treatment requires. But before that, it won't hurt to take a brief look at how practices compare with other social institutions that are related to practices—and partly made up of practices—but that aren't exactly practices themselves. This survey will be a further step in the process of understanding what a practice is, this time by "comparing and contrasting" rather than defining. It will also offer another clue to the importance of practices in making us who we are, since we will find—or at least I'll argue that we'll find—that these other social institutions are related to practices in crucial ways.

Let me turn, at the outset, to the idea of community. I want to start here for two reasons. First, understanding the relationship of practices to community will make the comparisons to civil society and to culture easier (in ways that will become clearer when we get to those concepts). Second, the issue of community is a compelling one in our public discourse these days. We currently hear laments for the loss of community from both the political left and the right. On the left, there is the concern that the dominance of multinational capitalism forces isolation upon individuals, an isolation that prevents them from seeing themselves as a part of a public community to which they have responsibilities and from which they can draw meaning. For many, multinational capitalism renders the space of traditional public political debate less significant, blunting people's ability to change their world as well as their ability to find a place in it.

Alternatively, the right worries that in our contemporary society, in which the value of anything is determined by people's willingness to pay for it, we have lost the traditional shared values that used to bind us together as a community. For these people, a common commitment to certain historically embedded values is the centerpiece of all community. Any change that militates against that commitment threatens the fabric of the community itself.

Near the end of the book, I'll return to these concerns. There is, it seems to me, something correct in the idea that our dominant capitalist order has helped to undermine important aspects of our lives. Not surprisingly, I will articulate what has been undermined in terms of practices. But for now I want only to illustrate the kinds of worries that have brought the issue of community forward in people's thinking about the world in which we live.

So what is a community, anyway? We often think about what we might call a "sense of community," which is something like a sense of belonging to some kind of social entity. The opposite of a sense of community is personal isolation. We may, then, be tempted to think of a community as whatever it is that binds us to other people in ways that prevent us from falling into a state of isolation. That's a fair start. But it doesn't tell us very much about what a community is. In trying to get an idea of what a community is, I think the best place to start—and here you will no doubt be shocked—is with the idea of practices.

I used to think, and even went so far as to publish the thought, that communities were simply practices or groups of practices. It seemed to me at that time that the only addition the term *community* offered to our language was that it allowed us to talk about groups of practices that had something in common—usually the people who participated in them—but that otherwise there was no difference between practices and communities. However, when I presented this idea publicly, I often was faced with a challenge that left me uneasy. Everyone can think of examples of practices that seem not to be amenable to the idea of community. One example that was thrown my way concerned those involved in the use of credit cards. Using credit cards is certainly a practice. But would we really want to say that there is, in any interesting sense, a community of credit-card users? Of course we can say that if we like, but something seems to be missing. If there is a community of credit-card users, that is a community in a very different sense from the community formed by those who worked for divestment from South Africa, or by those who are members of the same church.

What seems to be missing is the sense of community that attaches to people working for divestment or going to the same church, but that does not attach to credit-card users. Now in discussing this sense of community, we have to be careful. Not everybody whom we would want to call a member of a community feels the communal sense of belonging that I have labeled a "sense of community." Think, for example, of many adolescents who attend church only because their parents demand it of them. They are members of that particular community of churchgoers, but they don't have any of the sense of community that often comes with that membership. We can't, then, just say that a sense of community among all its members is a neces-

sary feature of community, since there may be members of a community who don't share that sense.

My own view is that what we are getting at with the idea of a sense
of community is not an emotional attachment but something a bit
different, something to do with the question of who we are. What
makes a community a community, as opposed to another kind of
practice (or group of practices), is that participation in that community
with others is generally indicative of a central feature of who each
participant is. In other words, what distinguishes communities from
other sorts of practices and groups of practices is that in communities,
people feel that they are expressing or realizing an important aspect of
who they are, that they do so in some sense with others who are also
expressing or realizing important aspects of who they are, and that
what often elicits a sense of community is the sharing of that expression or realization.

In order to make this point clearer, let me return to the church
example. What distinguishes churchgoing from using credit cards is
that for churchgoers, attending church expresses or realizes a significant aspect of who they are. To be a member of a particular church is
to say something important about who one is. That is not generally
true of people using credit cards. When I hand over my credit card to
the gas station attendant, I'm not expressing or realizing who I am in
any deep way—and certainly not in the way in which many people I
know express or realize themselves when they go to church.

Now before proceeding any further, I need to make sure that we're
clear about one thing. I've been saying all along that who we are is
largely determined by our practices. Am I now saying that who we
are is really only determined by those practices that would properly
form communities? No. First, I have made a distinction between the
idea of deep or significant features of who we are versus who we are
generally. Practices in which we engage that are not community practices may still be aspects of who we are, although those aspects are
often not as substantial as are community practices. I am a credit-card
user, and being a credit-card user does say something about me and
about my relationship to society, although it doesn't say as much as
my being a philosopher does.

Second, and more important, it is possible to be engaged in practices that are vitally constitutive of who one is but that are not really communities. To put the point in more logical terms: though all practices or groups of practices that we would want to call communities involve significant aspects of who one is, not all practices or groups of practices that we would *not* want to call communities *fail* to involve significant aspects of who one is. The reason for this is that for a practice or group of practices to be a community, there has to be a sharing of participation, a participation with others. But I can be a participant in a practice that is vitally constitutive of who I am without sharing my participation in that practice with others. For instance, I may be a writer who prefers my isolation, never attending writing conferences or other events that bring writers together into a community. (I suspect that there are many writers like that.) If so, I am still engaged in a practice that significantly determines who I am, but I am not a member of a community—even though that practice does have a community associated with it.

The upshot of this discussion is that while communities are significantly determinative of who we are, other practices also determine who we are, and sometimes they may be as significantly determinative of who we are as communities are.

Now someone might want to object to me here, saying that I've just contradicted something I said earlier. When I was explaining my initial resistance to seeing a sense of community as the necessary characteristic *of* a community, I said that part of that resistance was motivated by the idea that there could be an alienated member of a community, a member of a community who did not share a sense of community with the other members. But now I'm saying that participation in a community is a matter of expressing or realizing an important aspect of who one is alongside others. Now, why wouldn't the problem of the alienated community member be just as difficult for my take on community as it is for those who would want to see a sense of community as the central characteristic of community? Just as there can be members of a community who do not share any sense of community, couldn't there be reluctant members of a community who do not see that community as expressing or realizing significant aspects of who they are?

I'm going to defend the seemingly strange position that the answer to that question is *no*. Reluctant members of a community *do* have significant aspects of who they are expressed or realized in their participation in communities, even though they feel alienated from those communities. Let me give some reason to believe this apparently odd position. It seems to me that who we are is not simply a matter of who we feel we are. For instance, people who are mean-spirited rarely feel mean-spirited. They feel victimized, or misunderstood, or unlucky, or even unjustifiably generous. But they don't feel mean-spirited, at least not as a rule. There can be a difference between a person's sense of who he or she is and the fact of the matter about who he or she is. (Now who gets to decide what the fact of the matter is is a complex question. Let me duck it for my purposes here and just assume that I can get away with the claim that the final word on who someone is does not rest with that person alone.) If this is right, then by acting in certain ways a person can be expressing or realizing who he or she is without really wanting to do so.

And we can take this idea a step further. I would suggest that the alienation some people feel in the communities in which they participate lies precisely in the fact that they are being made into people they would rather not become. The cause of many people's alienation from the communities to which they belong lies in the concern, the *true* concern, that they are becoming the types of people they would rather not be. To argue for the contrary—that what's going on with an alienated member of a community is that he or she is being forced to act like someone he or she really isn't—doesn't capture the flavor of the resistance many alienated community members feel toward their community. Why is it that alienated churchgoers generally feel so much more alienated about going to church than credit-card users feel about using credit cards? The reason, I think, is that churchgoing is usually more formative for who one is. In attending church, one is becoming a certain kind of person whether one likes it or not. One may not *feel* like that kind of person, and that may be exactly what is bothersome. But the appropriate way in which to interpret that feeling and the alienation that comes from it is not to say that being a certain kind of churchgoer isn't who that person really is but that being that kind of churchgoer isn't who that person would really like to *be,* even though the person finds him- or herself being that person anyway: that's the source of the trouble.

It seems to me, then, that the problem that an alienated community member poses—for those who would like to define communities by relying on a sense of community—is not a problem for the account of community I'm offering here.

I'd like to touch quickly on another aspect of community before turning to the idea of civil society. And before doing that, let me point out that the account I have given of what a community is does not equate communities with practices in a wholesale way, but it does define community in terms of practices. Communities are just certain kinds of practices or groups of practices—those practices or groups of practices through which people share in expressing or realizing significant aspects of who they are. Seeing things in this way allows me to bring out another aspect of community in its relationship to practices. Depending on the significant characteristic of who people are that their participation in the community realizes, it is entirely possible to have one community that comprises several distinct practices. The reason for this is that you can have several different practices in which the same people are realizing or expressing the same characteristic of who they are.

Let me give an example. In some of my political work back in Pittsburgh, the same people would show up to different rallies: antiracism rallies, Palestinian rights rallies, divestment from South Africa rallies, and so on. Beyond that, we would also show up at different fund-raisers, different press conferences, and different civil disobedience actions. Granted, all of these activities could be thought of as involving the same practice. But not this: we would socialize together over dinner, eat at many of the same restaurants, and enjoy many of the same diversions together in our free time. Why? It wasn't just that we liked each other so much. In fact, some of us didn't particularly like some others of us. And it wasn't just that we didn't have anything better to do with our lives. On the contrary, most of us felt pretty pressed for time. Nevertheless, we felt both obliged and drawn to participation not only in the overtly political practices but also in at least *some* of the social ones as well. (Was it Oscar Wilde who said that the problem with socialism is that it takes too many evenings?)

As far as I can tell, the reason for our joint participation in these different practices is that the different practices were all expressions of a single aspect (or a cluster of closely related aspects) of who we thought ourselves to be. To put that aspect in a word, we were all *activists*. Through these different practices, we realized or expressed our being activists. We did so together, and through our doing so together confirmed for ourselves that we were indeed activists. Moreover, by doing so together, we *became* activists.

Now this isn't to say that one couldn't be an activist unless one attended dinners with other activists. Far from it. But these different practices became, for *us,* realizations or expressions of our activism. Although they were distinct practices, they converged on the same aspect of who each of us is—or was. The lesson here, then, is that although we can (and I think should) define communities in terms of certain kinds of practices, we don't want to say that there is a one-to-one correspondence between practice and community. Communities, although comprising practices, add a dimension to practices that makes the relation between the two more complex.

With that conclusion, let me turn from communities to civil society. The term *civil society,* which had fallen into disuse, has reemerged in public intellectual discussion in recent years. Much of this reemergence has to do with the rise, in political and social philosophy, of the movement called "communitarianism," which I'll consider in the last chapter of the book. Here I want to look briefly at a different manifestation of civil society's reemergence in public discussion. Several years ago, Robert Putnam wrote a short article entitled "Bowling Alone: America's Declining Social Capital." The article claimed that we in the United States are no longer participating in civil society, mostly because we're becoming increasingly isolated from one another by activities like watching television. I don't want to deal right now with the question of whether Putnam is right about either the lost participation or the reason for it. (Later, I'll agree with him in a certain way about lost participation, but ascribe it to a different cause.) For my immediate purposes, I want to look at the kinds of institutions and activities that he thinks are exemplary of civil society. After all, what we're trying to get hold of here is what civil society is and how it relates to practices.

Putnam lists a number of groups in his article that he thinks are part
of civil society: churches, social service agencies, veterans' groups,
fraternal orders, parent-teacher organizations, sports clubs and societies, literary groups, professional organizations, support groups, and
labor unions. Although he does not define the term *civil society,* it is
easy to see that all of these groups have several things in common.
First, they are voluntary in a way that having a job or a career isn't.
(In these groups, there might be someone paid to participate, such as
the facilitator of a support group. But the foundation of the group is
voluntary.) While one might argue that having a job is also voluntary—you could choose to starve—the voluntariness involved in join-
ing one of these groups is of a different order. Any pressure to join
will come from either oneself or one's social relations, and that kind of
pressure is usually more easily resisted than is the pressure of an empty
stomach.

Second, these groups are social, and social in a particular way.
Involvement in them is not a solitary activity; rather, it is a matter of
cooperative work alongside others who have the same goal. Moreover, this involvement takes the form of doing the same thing as
others, or something complementary, in order to achieve that goal. In
short, these groups are a matter of—you guessed it—practices.

Finally, all of these groups involve some kind of institutional structure. The institutional structure usually isn't the kind of structure you
find in either government or work. Nevertheless, all of these groups
have some form of institutional structure that helps to center the
practice in which the participants are engaged and that also helps to
keep it going. Not all practices need to have supporting institutional
structures; for instance, the practices of diary writing or of learning
Chinese cooking don't. But those practices tied up with what we call
"civil society" do require a more formal kind of institutional support.

With these three characteristics in hand—voluntariness, social practice, and institutional structure—we find ourselves in a position to
create a definition for the concept of *civil society.* We might define it
this way: civil society consists of a society's voluntary institutional
structures and their composite practices. That seems to capture the
idea we want and it immediately tells us how practices fit into the

picture. The practices of civil society are what occur by means of its voluntary institutional structures.

Here again, we can see that not all practices are the practices of a civil society. We can't subsume the idea of practices under the concept of civil society—nor subsume the idea of civil society under that of practices. We can't do the first because there are many practices that are not those of civil society. Think, for instance, of the many jobs that are not voluntary in the way that is necessary for civil society, but that still involve practices. All professions, and probably most jobs in general, fall into that category. Or, alternatively, think of how many practices there are that do not involve participating in some institutional structure. Touch football, roaming dinner parties, children's tag, informal literary groups: all of these are practices with no supporting institutional structure, and thus are not part of civil society. Moreover, some kinds of practices—despite the existence of voluntary institutional structures that might cover them—just happen to take place in a more informal way. Pickup games of soccer may take place without a league, but they still involve the kinds of rules and norms associated with practices as I have defined them. There are, then, many different practices that are not part of civil society.

Turning things the other way around: civil society is more than just a matter of practices. It is also a matter of institutional structure. Now, many practices do have supporting institutional structures, but having an institutional structure is not, as we have just seen, necessary for a practice. It is, however, necessary for something to be part of civil society. So, although civil society does involve practices, there is more to civil society than just those practices. As a result, just as we can't reduce the idea of practices to that of civil society, neither can we reverse the terms and reduce the idea of civil society to that of practices. Civil society, like community, is a matter of practices—but not only practices. In the case of community, there have to be certain kinds of practices before there is a community; in the case of civil society, there have to be certain kinds of institutional structures in order for the practice to be a part of civil society.

Let me address, finally, the relationship between practices and culture. This relationship is a little more tricky, because the word *culture* is a bit slippery. It can mean any one of at least several different things.

One thing it can mean is something like "the arts." In New York, we refer to the arts, and particularly to what are often called the high arts, using this term. (Actually, we don't use this exact term. We use another word somewhat like it: "culchuh.") In order to mark this particular meaning of the word, let me retain the term *culchuh* for culture in that sense.

A second meaning the word *culture* can have is more anthropological. In this case, "culture" is more or less equivalent to "society." For an anthropologist to study a culture is for him or her to study a given society or social grouping, usually bounded by certain geographical limits and a common language. For the sake of ease, let me coin the term *anthroculture* for this meaning of culture.

I'm not interested here in either culchuh or anthroculture. It's not that these aren't fascinating phenomena in their own right, or that they don't have anything to do with practices. On the contrary: the arts, indeed, are a matter of intersecting practices—and, in a different way, societies are too. That much should be clear from the discussion until now. But there is a third use of the term *culture* that is linked in an interesting way with practices and that might tell us a bit more about the kinds of relationships we have with one another.

To explain: "culture" can be said to mean something akin to what parents mean when they speak of their kids being in a "subculture." As far as I can tell, when people speak of others as being members of a subculture, what they mean is that those people are members of a culture different from their own. In the late 1960s and early 1970s, for instance, almost every person under the age of, say, twenty-five was said to be a member of "the subculture." In using this term, parents seemed to be implying that there was a mainstream culture of which almost everybody—and surely everybody with any sense—was a part. That mainstream culture accepted rivalry with the Soviet Union as a natural part of life and saw the profusion of consumer goods in our society as knockdown proof of our system's superiority to any form of socialism; if any member of mainstream culture opposed the slaughter that went by the name "the war in Vietnam," he or she had the decency not to say so. The subculture, of course, questioned all that. But the problem was that, at the time, the subculture was not so small. In fact, in cities like New York it was nearly universal in some form or another among young folks. And yet it was distinctly different from mainstream culture.

So if it's not size that makes a subculture a subculture, what is it? When we have the answer to that question, then we'll also have the answer to the question of what a culture (as distinct from culchuh and anthroculture) is. Let me suggest that the idea of a subculture in this sense is closely linked to that of a community. This, of course, is no surprise, since both subculture and community involve practices that have to do with people's sense of who they are. The difference between a community and a subculture, I suspect, is more a matter of degree than of kind.

What distinguishes a subculture from a community seems to be the number and kinds of practices that are shared and the concomitant sense of who one is that is given by that sharing. Members of a community (e.g., a church community) may be able to relate well to members of other church communities or to people who don't go to church. They can relate in a range of ways: through class identification, regionally accepted values, common interests, and so on. When it comes to religious issues, to be sure, a divide begins to open. But that divide can be circumnavigated if people want to do so. After all, except in rare cases, what binds people to one another isn't a single given commitment or set of values, but common participation in the multifarious aspects of social living.

Between different subcultures, however, or between what may (often a bit misleadingly) be called a subculture and the mainstream culture, matters are not so smooth. A subculture involves many aspects of a person's life and includes many practices that are alternative to those of the mainstream. It therefore makes contact with members of other subcultures more precarious. There is less in the way of shared practices and a shared sense of who one is, and consequently (as we'll soon begin to see) less in the way of shared values or a shared orientation toward the world. Intersubculture communication and relationships become more difficult. This is not to say that they are impossible. As I mentioned, the difference between community and culture is more one of degree than of kind. But when we speak of a subculture as opposed to a community, we usually do so with the recognition that there are communicative or relational difficulties present that wouldn't be if we were just talking about communities.

What holds for a subculture also holds for a culture. The difficulties of communication or relationship across subcultures are just the same across cultures—which is why the term *subculture* seems suspect. When we speak of multiculturalism, for instance, we mean trying to understand the world through eyes that see and engage with it in ways that are different from our own ways of seeing and engaging. Otherwise, there would be no need for multicultural perspectives; we could simply integrate the significant works of that other culture (now no longer a culture) into our own, using our own standards and values. So the view of a subculture I just gave holds equally true for a culture.

And inasmuch as cultures are extensions of communities, the composition of cultures by practices is much the same as the composition of communities by practices. The only difference between communities and cultures (and recall that we are not talking here about culchuh or anthroculture) is the qualitative and quantitative distinctness of the webs of practices that constitutes them.

To conclude, then: in this last section of this part of the book, I have tried to compare practices with other important social entities that are often the subjects of discussion and debate, and to show how practices are partially constitutive of each. We cannot eliminate the terms *community, civil society,* or *culture* in favor of the single term *practice,* since each word focuses on a particular dimension of our social lives. Nevertheless, the idea of practices plays an important part in each concept; to the extent to which we can come to a more nuanced understanding of practices, we will deepen our knowledge of those concepts as well. Although I won't say much more in the rest of this book about them, I will spend a lot of time trying to engage in a deepening of our concept of a practice. And on the basis of that deepening, I may lay the groundwork for understanding how things might go with community, civil society, and culture.

2   OUR PRACTICES AND OUR KNOWLEDGE

THINKING ABOUT KNOWLEDGE

So where are we?

At this point, I hope to have given you at least an initial sketch of the idea of practices and offered you some idea of why they may be important to who we are—and why thinking in terms of practices might give us a better sense of who we are than a couple of common alternative accounts. I also hope to have shown you how practices relate to other important social groupings.

What we don't have yet is much depth. I have remained on the surface of practices, not touching many of their core aspects or the more subtle ways in which they structure our lives. In order to move beneath the surface, I'll need to delve into important dimensions of who we are in order to see how the core aspects of practices accommodate them. If it turns out that thinking in terms of practices helps to explain these other aspects of who we are, and even gives us a better understanding of them than we would otherwise have, then we will have good reason to adopt the idea of practices as central to who we are.

I want to start this exploration with the idea of knowledge, and, in turn, start delving into the idea of knowledge by approaching what we think of when we think of the term *knowledge*. Knowledge, by itself, is a fairly abstract concept. It seems able to cover such disparate beliefs as "The sum of the angles of a triangle is always 180 degrees" and "I have a hangnail." What do these two beliefs have in common? What allows them both to fall under the same concept? As it will turn out, several things. But before we see the similarity in these beliefs, we first have to see that there is a difference between knowledge of the kind cited in these examples—knowledge that can be put into words—and something else that we would also want to call knowledge and that isn't so easily put into words. This difference has come to be called, in philosophy at least, the difference between "knowing-that" and "knowing-how."

Knowing-that is knowledge that can be put into words. For instance, you *know that* the sun will rise tomorrow; I *know that* I will not finish writing this book today; we both *know that* elephants are bigger than fleas. All of these knowings can be—in fact, just were—given linguistic form. To underscore the idea that knowings-that can be put into words, we might say that what it is that is known can have quotation marks around it. Take one example: "The sun will rise tomorrow" is something you know. Now since words are the kinds of things that quotation marks go around, and since knowings-that can have quotation marks put around them, we can conclude that knowings-that are matters of words. Or, to put the point another way, knowing-that concerns *claims,* while knowing-how does not.

Knowing-how concerns certain skills that one might be able to display but not necessarily be able to put into the form of a claim. Most people, for example, *know how* to ride a bike, but there are no particular words for *what* one knows when one knows how to ride a bike. If we tried to put quotation marks around it, we would be able to see the difference between the knowing-how that one has relative to bike riding and the knowing-that that one has relative to the sunrise. "Riding a bike," in quotation marks, is not even a claim, much less a bit of knowing-that, and doesn't compare with "The sun will rise tomorrow" as something that one can know. (In order to make sure that we're clear here, let's keep in mind that there is a difference between my knowing *how* to ride a bike and knowing *that* I can ride a bike. The second knowing can be put into words, but only the first one is a knowing-how.)

One might be tempted to mark the difference between knowing-that and knowing-how by saying that while the first is mental, the second is physical. That won't exactly work, though, and not just for the reason that the relations between the mental and the physical are a source of long-standing philosophical debate. The problem with that way of making the distinction is that there are plenty of different knowings-how that we would not readily classify as physical. Here's one. My five-year-old daughter is already a master of what the French call *savoir-faire*. She has an impeccable ability to go into a social situation and figure out how to relate to others in the best possible way. Part of this has to do with a precocious empathy with others. But beyond the empathy, she also possesses an uncanny sense of how to navigate social situations. Now this kind of *savoir-faire* is certainly a knowing-how, not a knowing-that. It cannot be put inside quotation marks or rendered in the form of a claim. But we wouldn't want to call it a purely physical knowing either. After all, it involves such skills as recognizing how people interact and what they are likely to feel. So we can't draw a distinction between knowing-that and knowing-how along an alleged divide between the mental and the physical. Rather, we'll have to maintain the original distinction—one between knowings that can be put into quotation marks (or in the form of claims) and knowings that involve certain skills and that can't be put in the form of claims.

Traditionally, philosophy has been much more concerned with knowing-that than with knowing-how. One of the reasons for this, a reason that I'll explore more deeply in a bit, has to do with the idea that for many philosophers, the point of studying knowledge has been to build up a body of certain and indubitable truths that can form the basis for all of our other beliefs. We would derive as much of the rest of our knowledge as possible from this body of truths. In order to get an idea of what these philosophers envisioned, picture our knowledge as a house that, in order to be as stable as possible, must have unshakable foundations. The philosophical project, then, would be to build the foundation out of unshakable claims upon which the rest of the house could rest securely.

This philosophical project, which can be said to be the common project of such philosophers as René Descartes, Kant, and perhaps even G. W. F. Hegel—to name a few of the luminaries—is called, not surprisingly, "foundationalism."

The foundations sought by foundationalist philosophers have to be knowings-that; they cannot be knowings-how. The reason that they have to be knowings-that is that the rest of the house of knowledge, in order to be connected to the foundations, is going to have to have the proper cement. And the proper cement here is inference: the inference from one claim to another—for instance, the inference from "That book is blue" to "That book is colored." (We'll see more— much more—on the idea of inference later.) Knowings-that allow for what are called "inferential relations," or inferences between various claims. Knowings-how do not. One cannot, strictly speaking, infer anything from the ability to ride a bike or to navigate smoothly through social situations or to sense the appropriate time to put a final offer on the table in negotiations.

To avoid confusion here, we need to recognize that one *can* infer something from knowing that one can, say, ride a bike. For instance, one can infer that the person who can ride a bike is older than six months. But, as I mentioned above, there is a difference between knowing how to ride a bike and knowing that one can ride a bike.

In any case, the guiding project of foundationalism among philosophers has led to the privileging, in the philosophical tradition, of knowing-that over knowing-how. I think that this privileging has had some unfortunate consequences, particularly in regard to practices. Practices involve not only knowings-that but also knowings-how.

Moreover, the knowings-how that they involve often serve as the basis for many of their knowings-that, in ways that I'll discuss momentarily. But since knowing-how has been neglected in the philosophical tradition, at least until recently, the role that practices play in our knowledge has also been neglected. When one sees the source of our knowledge in practices, the philosophical project of foundationalism itself comes under question. In fact, it no longer makes sense. But as long as we hold on to that project, we will be blind to the role of practices in what it is that we know and that we think we know.

I want to discuss the relation of practices first to knowings-how and then to knowings-that. But before doing so, let me pause before an objection that may have already occurred to some readers regarding these two types of knowledge.

Some people, noticing how different knowing-that is from knowing-how, may wonder why both should fall under the same general category: knowledge. Why are both of them forms of knowing? Aren't we talking about apples and oranges here? And if so, what reason is there that we should call them both the same thing (fruit, perhaps)? Shouldn't we just keep them separate, since one is a matter of claims and the other the very different matter of skills?

The short form of my reply to this objection is: "Whatever." I don't think much hangs on being able to make the case for both knowing-that and knowing-how as forms of the same thing, that same thing being knowledge. For those of you who would like to count them under one category, that's fine. But it's also fine not to do so. Since I will be keeping them separate as the discussion unfolds, there should be no difficulty there. If I were to offer a whole theory of what knowledge is, then I would have to come down on the question of whether both knowing-that and knowing-how are knowledge, and I would have to give a more full-blooded account of knowledge than I'm going to give. Fortunately for me, in order to draw the connections between practices and knowledge that I want to draw, I don't have to offer a full theory of knowledge. For my purposes, nothing is at stake here; either we have two components of knowledge, or two different things that happen to share some of the same letters.

With that, let me turn to the relation of practices to knowing-how. This discussion will be much shorter than the discussion concerning the relation of practices to knowing-that (although knowing-how will return in the context of knowing-that), in good part because philosophy has been much more concerned with knowing-that than with knowing-how. So, if my own presentation is going to be philosophically respectable, I've got to be able to engage these issues on the ground on which they've been engaged before. I'll follow the tradition, then, in focusing on knowing-that, but as we go, I'll point to some ways in which knowing-that seems to depend on knowing-how.

We can also spend less time on the relation between knowing-how and practices because this relation is very straightforward. Many of the knowings-how that we possess are skills that we either learn in order to participate successfully in practices or learn from exposure to practices in which we don't (or no longer) participate. Let me offer a couple of examples to illustrate what I mean.

Dancing is both a practice and one that involves a lot of knowing-how. It certainly qualifies as a practice, since it comprises social rules of dancing as well as non-rule norms of good and bad dancing, regularities of partner behavior, and goals of social interaction, physical fitness, and often artistic expression and/or sexual intimation—all of which interact to form the practice. As for knowing-how: just counting out the steps of a dance and moving your arms and legs in the prescribed ways may count as on the way toward dancing, but it ain't the real thing. (Don't I know.) Becoming a dancer requires you to know how to navigate the space of the dance floor, to anticipate the movements of your partner, and to express yourself in the desired ways to that partner (or partners or audience). This know-how is what one practices in order to become successful at the practice itself. (In this last sentence, let me note that I've used the term *practice* twice with distinct meanings.)

Generally, know-how is the mastery of something that requires practice (in the sense of study and repetition) in order to be good at a particular practice (in the sense that this book is exploring). Not all the time, though. Certain people have skills that will allow them to be good at particular practices without having to go through inordinate study and repetition. For instance, some people have natural athletic skills that make them good at many sports without their having to try terribly hard. (Of course, this natural skill usually only gets you so far without *any* study or repetition.) Other people, such as my daughter, have natural know-how in social situations; this know-how gives them an edge in practices requiring interpersonal skill without their having to try to figure out how others are seeing things from perspectives different from their own. But for the most part, being good at a practice *demands* practice, demands the development of a certain know-how that enables one to engage in the practice successfully.

Once the know-how is there, it leaves its mark on who one is. To stay with the example of dancing, the know-how that a long-term engagement with dancing brings can impress its stamp on a person's participation in other practices and in his or her life more generally. Some people who have had experience with dance are attuned to how others are moving their bodies and to the emotional states expressed by such movements, and they know how to interact with others in a nonlinguistic, bodily way. A person's know-how, then, does not necessarily wither with the end of participation in the practice that required the know-how; it can be carried on into other areas of a person's life.

When we see things in this way, we begin to understand how know-how is mostly caught up either (1) in the attempt to participate in practices successfully or (2) in the fallout from having participated in—or perhaps just having been exposed to—certain practices. Know-how is knowing how to do something, how to navigate the world in some particular way. It is a skill that one either develops or has naturally, and it allows one to accomplish certain ends. To the extent to which doing something, navigating the world in some particular way, and accomplishing certain ends are matters of engagements in practices, then so are various knowings-how. This is not, of course, to say that knowings-how are themselves practices. That wouldn't be the right way to put it. Rather, I want to put it this way: knowings-how are largely employed in the context of practices. Knowings-how are like the skills I discussed earlier when I called into question Schatzki's use of the term "dispersed practices." Knowings-how are not the practices themselves; rather, they are the abilities we try to hone in order to participate in those practices.

Once we recognize this point, however, another one follows right away. And the next point shows the deep relationship between knowing-how and practices. To the extent that knowings-how are employed in practices (and bear in mind that I haven't argued that they are *only* employed in practices, just largely so), then what kinds of knowings-how are relevant to a person depends significantly on how the practices in which that person participates are structured. That is to say, what a person needs to know how to do—as well as what constitutes better and worse know-how—is mostly given by the practices in which that person participates.

For example, part of the practice of doing philosophy—although it is certainly possible to be a philosopher without doing this—involves giving papers at conferences. Now giving papers at conferences requires a lot of know-how, as anyone who has heard a paper given by someone who doesn't have the know-how will readily confirm. Having something original to say is not enough. You have to know which points are likely to be misunderstood by the audience and therefore will need to be clarified. You have to know when to summarize and to figure out when a summary is going to be repetitious and boring. You have to know when to make a difficult philosophical move and when to lighten up. You have to know how to use your voice in order to emphasize certain points. You have to have a sense of what kinds of claims are going to be controversial and which claims you can count on your audience to let you get away with. All of this requires spending time in philosophical practice and, often, in conferences.

Now, consider for a moment not simply the kinds of know-how I have just listed, but also two further points. First, why are these particular skills, and not others, required for successful participation in this aspect of philosophical practice? Second, what kinds of specific considerations have to be taken into account at a particular moment in order to know how, for example, to sense which claims are and are not going to be controversial? When we see the answers to these two questions, we'll also see how the practice of philosophy helps dictate the kinds of skills that are going to count as philosophical know-how.

As for the philosophical importance of these particular skills: one of the goals of the practice of philosophy is to get some broad under-standing of our world and our place in it; another goal is to get a sense of how to act in that world. But philosophers have been considering these questions for a long time. And in doing so they have developed certain kinds of approaches and certain kinds of terminologies (and, yes, jargons). If you're going to give a paper at a philosophy confer-ence, it's worth knowing about these approaches and these terminolo-gies for at least two reasons: first, so that you don't make some kind of philosophical mistake that has been recognized as a mistake for hun-dreds of years; and second, so that you can reach your audience in the right way. Reaching your audience in the right way is important. Think of what happens if you have something truly original to say, but you pass it over quickly or fail to point out its significance or neglect to give good reasons to back it up. The likelihood is that your argument will be dismissed or ignored. Having the know-how in giving a philosophical paper avoids all that. But having the know-how entails having an understanding of what the state of the practice is and how one ought to fit oneself into that state in the appropriate way.

That leads directly to the other question I raised earlier: What kinds of considerations have to be taken into account at a particular mo-ment in order to have the appropriate philosophical know-how to deliver a successful paper at a conference? The answer to the question will depend, of course, on the state of the practice at that moment. And that, precisely, is the point. Appropriate know-how is largely dictated by the state of the practice: the kinds of things you have to know in order to have the right know-how are given by the practice itself. This does not mean that there aren't certain kinds of know-how that remain constant (such as how to emphasize a controversial point). But the kinds of points that are controversial, and the kinds of empha-ses needed by specific controversial points, will change with the state of the practice. And with those changes come changes in the specific content of what one must know how to do in order to be successful in giving a philosophical paper.

If, for instance, I deliver a paper arguing that we ought to stop thinking that all systems of morality require a belief in God, I'm going to be laughed out of court. Why? Because in the current state of philosophical practice, almost nobody believes that systems of morality require a belief in God. It's just not controversial, and so there is no need to defend it. (But if I deliver a paper claiming that morality does require a belief in God, now I'm saying something controversial. The tricky part, of course, lies in being able to back up my view with the kinds of reasons a philosophical audience can accept as good ones.)

None of what I have said is meant to imply that the current state of any practice *dictates* the kind of know-how that is relevant to that practice. The relationship between practices and know-how is not a one-way street, running from the needs of the practice to the character of good know-how. That street runs two ways. The kinds of know-how people have at a particular moment might well help determine the shape of a given practice as well. For instance, the limits of people's ability to respond creatively to one another through written communication may constrain (as well as dictate the flavor of) many of the practices involving relationships that are formed through electronic media. My point, then, is not that practices dictate know-how but rather that know-how arises within and responds to the concerns of specific practices. This arising within and responding to does not discount the ability of various knowings-how to shape the contours of the practices within which they come into play. (When we get more deeply into knowing-that, we will see a corresponding point: the fact that knowledge occurs within practices does not mean that practices dictate knowledge. The relationship is more complex.)

So far, I have been discussing the relationship between practices and know-how. I've been trying to make the case that know-how, as a form of knowledge (or, for those who like their knowledge to be solely knowing-that, as a form of something that is often good to have), is intimately bound up with practices. Know-how is usually either deployed by someone in the context of various practices—in order to be a successful participant in those practices—or results from having participated in one or another practice. I want to turn now from knowing-how to the more complex issue of knowing-that. As we will see, the tortured philosophical history of knowing-that will bring us down a number of unusual roads. But I hope that at the end of those roads, we begin to see our knowledge in a renewed light, one that shows the intimate ties between our practices and our lives.

KNOWING-THAT: A BRIEF HISTORY

If we're going to tackle the thorny issue of knowing-that, the best starting point is probably with a short background history of the concept. In order to keep the terminology easier, I'll substitute the word *knowledge* for the term *knowing-that,* since "knowledge" is more in keeping with the terminology of philosophical history. However, let's remember—and every once in a while I'll call attention to this—that it's knowing-that and not knowing-how that we're talking about here. A brief history of knowledge will help to show the kinds of concerns philosophers have inherited and also the kinds of perspectives against which current views of knowledge unfold. (Stated otherwise, a short history of knowledge will give us some know-how in navigating the philosophical field in this area.) Now we could start that background history as far back as Plato, but we won't. Fortunately for us, we don't need to go that far. Instead, what I'm going to propose (and then, since I am also the author, accept) is to start with René Descartes. In fact, most of our current concerns about knowledge derive from his thought, and so this won't be a bad place to begin.

From Descartes, I'll jump to one of his twentieth-century heirs, Edmund Husserl. And from there, the next stop will be several philosophers who have reacted in different ways against the tradition that runs from Descartes to Husserl: Thomas Kuhn, Hans–Georg Gadamer, and Ludwig Wittgenstein. As with the earlier parts of the book, this section will presume no knowledge of any of these philosophical figures. What I'm trying to offer here is a picture of some select strains in the history of philosophical approaches to knowledge, so that I can set the stage for a discussion of the relation of knowledge to practices.

What Descartes wanted to do was to give some foundation to our knowledge (here I refer to *foundation* in the sense that we saw a while ago). Now Descartes did not distinguish between knowing-how and knowing-that, and in fact, like many philosophers, he seemed to consider knowing-that as the only kind of knowledge there is. The problem Descartes faced was that in the mid-1600s, the period during which he wrote, knowledge (in the sense of knowing-that) seemed to derive from some sort of ecclesiastical authority. The church was the

repository of knowledge; if the church said it, it was true. For Descartes, as for many of us, the word of the church was not good
enough. (Aware of the church's treatment of Galileo, though, he did
not put matters in quite that way.) What he sought, then, was a
foundation for knowledge that did not rely on ecclesiastical authority.

It's important to be clear here on exactly what Descartes wanted,
because that's what sets the stage for the whole philosophical tradition
about knowledge that he initiated. Descartes's goal was no less than a
firm foundation for all of our knowledge, a foundation of truths so
certain that they could not be coherently denied; such a foundation
would serve as the basis for building up the rest of our knowings-that.
The term that is often used for this approach, *foundationalism,* is not
misapplied here. In order to understand his project, recall that the
truths for which he was looking are the foundation of the house of
knowledge. If that foundation is shaky, the rest of the house could
come tumbling down. But, if the foundation is strong, we can build
upon it with confidence.

In order to serve as a strong foundation, the truths Descartes sought
needed to have at least two qualities. First, they had to be indubitable;
that is to say, they had to be such that no reasonable person could
deny them. They had to be immune to reasonable doubt. Second,
they had to serve as a real foundation for other kinds of truths. The
kinds of truths Descartes sought could not just be some marginal
truths with no real connection to our experience or our lives. Otherwise, they would be a foundation upon which no house could be
built. So the truths he wanted to find for the foundation had to be
able to serve as building blocks for other kinds of truths that would be
worth knowing.

We don't need to look in detail here at the way in which he tried
to perform this feat, since the part that is relevant for us is his goal
rather than his attempt to reach it. But, briefly, this was his strategy:
he figured that if he could prove that everything that he could conceive "clearly and distinctly" was true, then that would do the trick.
It's easy to see how. Sometimes you have a clear idea of what is going
on; sometimes not. If your clear ideas were true—in other words, if
they were instances of knowledge—then you'd have a lot of knowledge to go on. So Descartes's move was to try to put as the corner-

stone of his foundation for knowledge the claim that everything one clearly and distinctly conceives is true. (The word "conceives" is mine, not Descartes's. If it sounds a bit slippery, it's meant to; there's a fair amount of debate about what kinds of things could, according to Descartes, be the object of clarity and distinctness.)

In order to establish that cornerstone, Descartes tried to prove two other things: that God exists, and that God is not a deceiver. He felt that if he could prove those two things, then he could conclude that God would not give something to people's consciousness clearly and distinctly that would be wrong. That, after all, would be deceptive. So he offered a proof of the existence of God (two proofs, actually), and then a proof of the nondeceptiveness of God, and from there concluded that everything he clearly and distinctly conceived must be true.

Now if it seems to you as though there might be a hole or two in this whole strategy, you're not alone. Many people have made it their business to discover holes in Descartes's strategy, right from the day Descartes published his thoughts. But a glance at the goal and the strategy reveals what is important for our purposes: the structure of foundationalism. Foundationalism always seeks to place our knowings-that on some bedrock of indubitable truth upon which the rest of our knowings-that can be supported. That's what Descartes was on about, and that's what every foundationalist since him has been on about.

It is worth calling attention, at this point, to the fact that if knowledge is conceived on the foundationalist model, it doesn't necessarily have very much to do with practices. What Descartes and other foundationalists sought were universal truths—claims that people *had* to ratify, *had* to assent to, regardless of the practices in which they were engaged or the reasons with which they were used to dealing. (So insofar as we think of beliefs and reasons as caught up in practices, and insofar as foundationalism calls for truths which lie beyond the reasons and beliefs of particular practices, then foundationalism will have little use for practices in its view of the structure of knowledge.)

For better or worse, foundationalism held sway in philosophical approaches to knowledge until at least the middle of this century. This is not to say that all philosophers were foundationalists. Many well-known philosophers, such as David Hume, were not. But the dominant tradition in *epistemology*—the theory of knowledge—was foundationalist. This had a profound effect on philosophy itself, since for many philosophers the question of the status of knowledge has been the central question that philosophy has needed to answer. And so the embrace of foundationalism skewed the entire field of philosophy in a certain direction for several centuries: the direction of looking for bedrock truths upon which to build philosophical systems.

A more contemporary example of foundationalism is found in the work of Edmund Husserl, a German philosopher who mostly wrote during the first third of the twentieth century. Husserl, like Descartes, sought a foundation of indubitable knowings-that upon which the various sciences, by grounding themselves in this foundation, could gain stability. Husserl thought it a scandal that the sciences, as far as they had advanced in giving us empirical knowledge, still lacked a solid theoretical foundation upon which they could rest. And he thought that it was the task of philosophy, and his task in particular, to give the sciences that solid theoretical foundation.

Husserl's approach to knowledge was, in many ways, very close to that of Descartes. (In fact, the title of one his most well-known books is *Cartesian Meditations*.) The key difference between them lay in the fact that by the twentieth century, the foundation for knowledge could no longer lie with God. Foundationalism had to stand or fall upon nontheological grounds. (There is a neat irony in the fact that it was probably Descartes, more than anyone, who laid the groundwork for the rejection of theology in philosophical theories of knowledge, even though he himself had recourse to God in his own work. By rejecting the blind appeal to ecclesiastical authority, Descartes set in motion a process that went much further than he could have envisioned.) Like Descartes, Husserl felt that the proper foundation for knowledge lay in the clarity and distinctness of human conceiving; unlike Descartes, though, he believed that the guarantee for that clarity and distinctness had to come from human consciousness itself, not from a power outside consciousness (i.e., God). Human consciousness had to be self-supporting.

We need not linger over the details of Husserl's strategy for developing a foundation. It is, in many ways, far more complex than

Descartes's, and the point of looking at Husserl is more one of seeing the continuity of foundationalism than of trying to navigate the details of his approach. (Scholars of contemporary philosophy will immediately raise the charge of oversimplification. Guilty.) Here then, in brief, was Husserl's strategy: like Descartes, Husserl wanted to found knowledge in something indubitable. What he noticed was that there was something indubitable about our experiences—for example, our perceptual experiences—if we take those experiences in a certain way. Although it might be possible that there is, say, no computer in front of me at this moment, it is certainly true that I am having an experience of the kind that people have when there are computers in front of them. There may be no computer here, but I am nevertheless having what we might call a "computer-experience," just as you, reading this later, are having a "book-experience," even if by some bizarre twist of fate there really is no book in front of you. (Sounds strange, I know, but bear with me. Philosophers have been in much stranger places.)

Otherwise put, it is possible (although, granted, *extremely* unlikely) that there is no book in front of you at this moment; maybe you're hallucinating. But it is impossible that, as you read this and think of yourself as reading a book, you are not having an experience of the kind that I am calling a "book-experience": that is, an experience of yourself as reading a book. You might be wrong about the book being there, but you can't be wrong about the experience itself.

Now Husserl thought that since our knowledge was ultimately built out of our experiences, our experiences—or better (though more awkward), our *experiencings*—were the bedrock upon which a foundationalist theory of knowledge should be built. It was in turning away from our beliefs about objects in the world, and turning toward our experiencings of what we believe to be objects in the world, that we would find the key to what was indubitable in our knowings-that.

One might be tempted—and, really, should be tempted—to ask the question of how these experiencings provide a real foundation for what is in the world. How, after all, does what happens in my mind give me any certainty as to what is going on in the world? That is surely the right question, but to answer it would take many pages and the kind of philosophical depth that we really don't need for our purposes. Suffice it to say that Husserl did try to answer that question, and tried to do so without leaving the realm of the mind or relying on God. In other words, he tried to build his foundation for the correctness of what appears indubitable to human consciousness without leaving the realm of human consciousness. He hoped to make human consciousness self-supporting, and in turn make human consciousness the support for all other knowledge, including the knowings-that that occur in science.

Efforts like Husserl's to construct a foundationalist theory of knowledge have continued to this day. They have, however, become suspect. The reasons for doubt are numerous and far-flung, but they are enough to put the foundationalist project under a cloud. As a result, other approaches to knowledge have arisen, approaches that see knowledge in terms other than that of a bedrock with supporting layers. It will be handy to have the foundationalist approaches to knowledge in the background in order to see what these more recent approaches are reacting against. But one thing seems clear: these other approaches converge upon the idea that knowledge (knowing-that, not just knowing-how) is more a matter of practices than of anything else. This convergence on the idea of practices is not there consciously in many of these approaches—but, in retrospect, it seems to offer the best way to understand them. So, before turning to my own take on the relationship between knowledge and practices, I want to continue this brief history a little further by glancing at three thinkers whose very different approaches to knowledge have pointed to the idea that knowledge (as well as knowing-how, and therefore knowing in general) is something that happens in the context of practices.

The first of these thinkers is Thomas Kuhn, whose book, *The Structure of Scientific Revolutions,* is arguably the most influential book of philosophy written in the twentieth century (although it is also arguably something other than a book of philosophy.) Kuhn is not *chronologically* the first of the three thinkers I want to consider. But he offers the easiest way in, in terms of summarizing his thought.

The Structure of Scientific Revolutions reacts against the prominent view of the day (the late 1950s and early 1960s) among philosophers writing in the United States and Britain that science was the paradigm of knowledge. Although calling this prominent view "foundationalist" would, at least in some cases, be a stretch, it would not be a stretch to say that science—and especially physics—held pride of place for most U.S. and British philosophers; its position was closely analogous to the place that God held for Descartes and human consciousness did for Husserl. Science was, for them, the model of inquiry. If inquiry did not meet the kinds of high standards that science set, then we could not get any knowledge out of it.

Kuhn's work went a long way toward undercutting this view. But he didn't undercut it by casting around for some other kind of inquiry that would have the respectability of science. Instead, he worked the other way around. He showed that scientific work wasn't nearly so lofty as many philosophers thought it was. Scientists, like the rest of us, spend most of their time working in situations in which they take a certain context and framework for granted, and they do what they do within the parameters defined by that context. In the scientists' case, what is taken for granted are the overarching views that are current in the field. In physics, for example, Newtonian mechanics once set the parameters for physical inquiry. Now either quantum mechanics or Einsteinian theory does. And most scientists design experiments whose goal is to extend in small ways the knowledge that we possess from within the different scientific frameworks.

That kind of work is not so different, in its way, from work that people in other professions do. Lawyers, for instance, rarely set out to change the current interpretation of constitutional law. (Some do, but most don't.) Instead, they take a case here and a case there, trying to win them on the basis of the current understanding of the law's implications. It may turn out that some case starts to raise questions about that current understanding. And, if enough cases like that are raised (or, more rarely, if a single case raises enough different questions on its own), the current understanding of the law's implications will change. But that is not the normal run of things in law, or in most professions.

And it isn't in science either.

Overarching scientific theories generally change, when they change, because repeated attempts to comprehend our world on the basis of those theories lead to frustration. A single anomalous result, unless it is really anomalous, won't motivate change. There are usually ways in

which to fiddle with big overarching theories in order to accommodate anomalies. But when enough anomalies arise, there is a scientific
crisis. At that point, competing theories come to the fore, each vying
for acceptance. And the result of that crisis is often the acceptance of a
new overarching theory or group of theories, which in turn provides
a new context within which a science operates. Then people go back
to their labs and construct their experiments within the new context,
which lasts until the next crisis.

One of the things that is interesting about this take on science
(which represents only part of what Kuhn argued, but perhaps the
most lasting part) is that scientists—whether constructing experiments,
reporting on them, or speculating on their implications—don't start
from what we might call "epistemic scratch." That is to say, they
don't start as if nobody had ever done a scientific experiment before,
and as if therefore they had to provide not only the experiment but
the entire context for understanding it. When you think about it,
starting like that would be hopeless. (Imagine trying to explain what
science is to people who base their entire system of knowledge on a
belief that events in the world are a product of the whimsy of fickle
gods.) Instead, they construct and interpret experiments according to
the context in which they find themselves. Sometimes their experiments challenge that context, in which case they either need to perform some more experiments or to start trying to discover what might
be wrong with the context. But usually the context provides a more
or less adequate framework within which to operate: more adequate,
if there are fewer or smaller anomalies, and less adequate if there are
more or greater anomalies.

But what is this context?

It has to do with scientists in a certain field performing experiments, in cooperation or in competition with other scientists, in order
to extend or deepen the range of scientific knowledge in that field. In
short, it has to do with particular scientific practices. What Kuhn
called to people's attention is that science happens in the context of
scientific practices. And we may also read him as calling to our attention that what we often call our knowledge occurs in the context of
our practices. Although we are often tempted to think of knowledge
as something that floats above or outside our daily immersion in

practices, it isn't. It's closely tied to those practices. Although, as we'll see, it isn't exactly correct to say that knowledge is relative to practices—in the sense that the state of a practice at a given moment determines what is or isn't known—it is exactly correct to say that knowledge happens in the context of practices. The difference between these two, which may sound identical at the moment, will take some time to unfold. But the more immediate point I want to press here is that Kuhn is one of the first philosophers to recognize (even if he didn't put it in these terms) that knowledge is inseparable from practices. That, of course, is the theme of this part of the book, and it is to Kuhn's credit that he saw it before most other people did and that he was able to document it in the area of knowledge that would seem most resistant to it: science.

Another philosopher writing around the same time as Kuhn also saw the connection between knowledge and our daily involvements with the world. The German thinker Hans-Georg Gadamer, a student of the famous (and infamous) philosopher Martin Heidegger, published his major work, *Truth and Method,* in 1960, just two years before Kuhn's *The Structure of Scientific Revolutions.* In this book, Gadamer laid out his own view of the philosophical approach known as *hermeneutics,* which might broadly be defined as the theory of interpretation. Gadamer's view was that it is a mistake to think of knowledge (knowing-that, but also knowing-how) as something that occurs outside the traditions in which we are brought up and through which we are taught to see the world. Instead, we should see knowledge as something that occurs in our interaction with the world by means of these traditions.

What Gadamer struggled against—and what Descartes and Husserl were struggling *for*—was the idea that there could be a pure standpoint, untainted by our traditions and our prejudices, from which any knowings-that could be had. Descartes and Husserl sought cosmic assurance that some kind of knowledge could form a foundation of certainty that would anchor the project of understanding ourselves and the world, a knowledge that would avoid the uncertainties that arise from our limited ability to understand the world through daily interaction. Gadamer denied that there was any such kind of pure knowledge. He argued forcefully that in order for there to be knowledge there had to be language, and that language always occurs in the context of traditions in which viewpoints develop, social relations form, and individual lives unfold.

The image Gadamer used for the idea that knowledge occurs within the context of traditions and their orientations and prejudices is that of the hermeneutic circle, an image he borrowed from Heidegger. The idea of the hermeneutic circle is that understanding always comes from within an already formed circle of previous understanding. In order to understand something, you have to have a context of understanding, a context that is given by the language and traditions in which your understanding occurs. Now Gadamer, like Heidegger, refused to admit that the hermeneutic circle implies that you can only learn what you already know. In other words, both denied that the circle was a vicious circle. The reason the circle is not vicious is that the circle itself changes with the new kinds of understandings—for our purposes, the new kinds of knowings-that—that it permits.

Let me give an example here. There is a book that has just been published that is causing a stir. It's by Judith Rich Harris, and it's called *The Nurture Assumption*. Harris claims that our current assumption that a child's development is the product of genetics and parental care is false. She argues that it is not so much parents as it is peers who contribute to the nongenetic aspect of a child's development. I don't want to argue over the merits of the case she makes; that isn't my point. I do want to draw our attention to the fact that Harris's argument is made within the context of the hermeneutic circle. She started, as she herself writes, by believing that the important nongenetic aspect of a child's development was parental care. But, as she tried to square that view with a number of psychological, sociological, and ethnological studies, it didn't hold up. So eventually she abandoned it in favor of one she thinks is better.

Consider what's going on here. Harris starts from within a context—the hermeneutic circle—that provides her with a framework for understanding childhood development. When she comes to question that context, it is not because she jumps wholesale into another context. Rather, it's because some aspects of that context don't seem to fit with others. That forces a rethinking of some (but not all) of the terms of the context itself. Should her theory prove compelling, it will

change the terms of the context—in other words, change the contours of the hermeneutic circle—and provide another circle (or better,
a redrawing of the original circle) through which others will come to
understand childhood development.

At no point, however, does Harris abandon everything she has
learned. It's hard even to imagine how that would happen. Instead,
she operates from within the parameters of her context, even when
she is questioning some of those parameters. That, in Gadamer's view,
is how knowledge has to occur. Knowledge must be capable of being
put in the form of words, as I argued earlier in this part of the book:
to know-that is to know that x is the case. And language is not a
neutral medium for our thoughts. It has its own orientation and even
its internal tensions, which depend on such factors as the history
and geography of the people who speak it. So rather than think of
knowings-that as little mirrors of the world that reflect the world to us
but do not reflect any of us back to ourselves, we must think of them
as claims that arise within language—the language of the ongoing,
historically situated lives of those who speak it. As I have emphasized,
this idea does not imply that those claims can only repeat the prejudices of those whose language it is. What it does imply, however, is
that knowledge must be thought of as occurring within our traditions
and prejudices, rather than outside them.

It is a short step from the idea of traditions and their prejudices to
the idea of practices. Although we would not want to equate traditions with practices, we would probably come close to the mark if we
equated traditions with cultures. And we have already seen how close
culture is to practices. We can already glimpse what I will be arguing
shortly: that practices are the sites of knowledge. When Gadamer talks
about understanding occurring within a tradition, one of the ways in
which to take this talk—and I think it is the right way—is to recognize that he is talking about knowing-that (and, in Gadamer's case, we
can probably throw in knowing-how as well) and telling us how it
arises in the context of our historically situated, socially normatively
driven, goal-directed behavioral regularities. In short, our practices.
Practices, after all, do have their own traditions and, as we have
already seen, involve us in ways of being and looking that form the
basis for much of our interaction with the world.

So far, we've spent this historical overview looking at two thinkers that are representative of the philosophical tradition regarding knowledge (in the sense of knowing-that) and two that have helped contribute to the current rethinking of knowledge. I have also claimed that the latter two can fruitfully be seen as endorsing the recommendation that we conceive of knowledge as something that arises within the context of practices. The third practice-oriented thinker that I want to discuss is Ludwig Wittgenstein. I won't spend a lot of time on him at the moment. The reason for this is not that Wittgenstein is a marginal character (far from it) or that he does not play an important role in these reflections (further still). Rather, it's the opposite.

My attempt to situate knowledge in the context of practices is so indebted to Wittgenstein that to offer more than a quick summary of his work and then go into my own view would be repetitive. Many of his most important points about knowledge appear in the pages that follow, and many that are not his can be seen as deriving from thoughts he developed. So all I want to do in advance of my own work is to make a few preliminary observations that you might want to treat as small talk in the foyer while you're taking off your coat and getting ready to sit for some longer conversation in my living room. (The image works better, I guess, if you're a really patient listener.)

Wittgenstein, whose writings preceded those of both Kuhn and Gadamer, spent the early part of his philosophical career trying to build a view of language and of knowledge that is probably best categorized as foundationalist. He wanted to show the ways in which language acts as a mirror of the world, giving us basic phrases and sentences that hook directly onto the world and from which we can construct the rest of our knowledge. Later, he came to reject this view, and he tried to rethink the ways in which language relates to the world and the implications of that for our knowledge—both our knowing-how and our knowing-that. His later work is never presented in a systematic form. (In fact, none of it was published during his lifetime.) Rather, it consists of notes and aphorisms from which philosophers have tried to produce a broader philosophical perspective. Although it's difficult to figure out the perspective—and I'll be the first to admit that my own take on Wittgenstein is only one of at least several possible takes—it is not impossible to derive a coherent philosophical viewpoint.

In broad outline, Wittgenstein began to think that language should not be treated as a single whole, but rather as a set of locally centered systems that he called "language-games." Language-games have their own rules and non-rule norms for the kinds of sentences or phrases that will count as justifiable or meaningful or permissible. When we move away from the model of language as a seamless whole and begin to think about language-games, we stop trying to ask how it is that language hooks onto or somehow reflects the world. Instead, we ask questions like this: What kinds of "forms of life" (Wittgenstein's term) do our language-games promote and what kinds of knowings— both how and that—can be had through them?

The move from seeing language as a seamless whole to seeing it as tied up in language-games, then, is a move from a foundationalist orientation to a practice orientation. We abandon questions about *the* way in which language relates to the world, as though there were one key that, when we discovered it, would allow us to open all of the important philosophical doors. Instead, we recognize that there are many keys, that those keys not only open out onto the world but also open onto our own lives and activities, and that it may be difficult (or even impossible) at times to tell the extent to which a door we have opened is a door into the world or into us, since our own views of the world come from the practices and lives in which we are immersed.

Now when Wittgenstein argued that we should think of language in terms of language-games rather than as a seamless whole, he was not arguing that none of us speak the same language, as though there weren't a language called English which we could all under-stand. What he was arguing—a point I'll spend some time on soon enough—is that the recognition that a group of people speaks the same language does not tell us very much about the people's lives or knowledge. If we want to know what people believe and how they act, we need to turn (among other places) to the specific uses of language in which they are engaged. And those specific uses of lan-guage occur in language-games.

If, for example, a person is a psychological counselor, the use he or she makes of language will be very different from the use made by a brain surgeon. For the first, statements offered by clients are symptoms of different kinds of psychological states. For the brain surgeon, by contrast, statements offered by patients are seen as symptoms of certain brain states. Now the brain states seen by the surgeon and the psychological states seen by the counselor may match up in some interesting ways. (The issue of the relation of the mind and body is probably something to be avoided here.) But even if they do, the kinds of claims that psychological counselors and brain surgeons are willing to endorse on the basis of statements offered to them are very different. The statement "I have a headache," for instance, might indicate a psychological problem of some sort to a counselor; to a brain surgeon it could be symptomatic of a brain lesion. That difference can be traced, in ways we will see, to the differences in the practices in which the two are engaged.

So when Wittgenstein said that language is caught up in language-games, we should not take him to be denying that two speakers of English are actually speaking the same language. Rather, we should take him as having believed that the roles played by language in people's lives require a more fine-grained understanding than just an awareness of which language people speak. They require an understanding of the uses to which that language is being put in the context of specific language-games.

The Wittgensteinian thoughts that I have been sharing with you here provide us with a framework within which I want to develop a view of knowledge that links knowledge with practices. But these thoughts also are in keeping with Kuhn's idea that science is a matter of practical engagements and Gadamer's idea that knowledge occurs within the context of historically situated traditions. In response to the work of Wittgenstein, Kuhn, Gadamer, and many others like them, philosophy has, over the course of the twentieth century, moved away from the foundationalist picture of knowledge and toward a more practice-oriented picture. In what follows, I want to offer a sketch of how knowledge looks from a practice-oriented point of view, and to delineate how that point of view shows various forms of knowledge to be deeply connected to who we are.

WHAT IS KNOWLEDGE (AS IN KNOWING-THAT)?

A venerable tradition in philosophy (and what are philosophical traditions, if not venerable?) traces a certain definition of knowledge back
at least as far as Plato. In that tradition, knowledge—of the knowing-
that variety—is defined as *justified true belief*. Three parts: justification,
truth, and belief. If, for instance, a person can be said to know that
most elected public officials are slimeballs, three things have to be
true. First, that person must *believe* that most elected public officials are
slimeballs. After all, how can you be said to know something if you
don't even believe it? Second, it has to be *true* that most elected
officials are slimeballs. You certainly can't be said to know something
that's false, so knowledge requires truth. Third, that person must be
justified in believing that most elected officials are slimeballs. That is to
say, he or she must have a reason to believe it; it can't just be a good
guess.

Let me linger for a moment over this third element of the definition, justification. As it turns out, justification is the most important
element for my own account. What the idea of justification adds to
true belief in getting us to knowledge is that knowledge can't be a
matter of chance. If, for example, I believe that the New York Giants
are going to win the Super Bowl this year, but I don't know any of
the players on the team, I don't know how they've done in previous
years, I have no idea of the coach's name—much less his record—and
I'm not even clear on the rules of football, then even if the Giants do
win the Super Bowl, we'd hesitate to say that I *knew* that they were
going to win. Oh, maybe *I* would say something like, "I knew it, I
knew it." But would I really have known it? Or would it just be a
good guess? Maybe I'm from New York (I am), and maybe I just like
the blue color of the uniforms (I do), and maybe I don't even know
the names of any other teams (okay, I'm making that part up), so I
pick the Giants to win. It might turn out that I'm right, but most of
us would agree that being right in this case wasn't a matter of knowing. To be said to know something, you've got to be able to give a
reason for it. What kind of thing counts as a reason we'll discuss in a
bit; for the moment, all I want to establish is that it can't just be a
matter of luck.

Having said this much in regard to the traditional definition of knowledge, let me call our attention to two points. First, not everybody in philosophy defines knowledge in this way. Recently, a profusion of uses of the term *knowledge* has arisen that is closely tied to the specific concerns of specific philosophical approaches, rather than to any general consensus on the use of the term. I have no particular difficulty with this profusion, as long as it is understood—as it usually is—that in using the term *knowledge* idiosyncratically, no claim is being made upon the philosophical tradition generally associated with knowledge. I'll keep with the traditional view, since it suits our purposes well and does get at what it is that happens when we speak in a day-to-day way about knowing something.

The second point is that there are difficulties with the definition of knowledge as it stands. The difficulties may be rather exacting, but they're probably at least worth recognizing. The philosopher Edmund Gettier pointed out that there are examples of justified true belief that we would probably not want to call "knowledge." For example, suppose that a person were sitting in a room that was dark except for one lit candle. Suppose the person developed a belief that there was a lit candle five feet away from him or her. Suppose it were true that there was a lit candle five feet away from him or her. Suppose that the basis upon which the belief was formed was what seemed to be a visual impression of a candle five feet in front of him or her. So far, so good: we have belief, we have truth, and we have justification.

But now, suppose that the lit candle was *not* five feet in front of him or her but five feet to the side, and through a sophisticated use of mirrors, it just *appeared* to be five feet in front. (Bear in mind that the belief being considered here is not that there is a candle five feet *in front* of one but a candle five feet *away* from one.) We still have belief, truth, and justification, but in this case they don't seem to be matched up in quite the right way. The reason for this is that the justification for the belief doesn't seem to match up cleanly with its truth. The belief is true, to be sure, and justified as well (given the evidence of the person's senses, he or she had adequate reason to believe that there was a candle five feet away). But in this case the truth of the belief is *not based on* its justification; instead, it's based on the circumstance that the justification, which could have led to the wrong belief, just happened to coincide with the truth of the belief. After all, the justification could just as well have led to the false belief that there was a candle five feet *in front* of one.

For a number of years, philosophers spilled a lot of ink trying to reply to examples like this one. What they sought was the other, fourth condition that had to be in place in order for there to be knowledge. What must be added to belief, truth, and justification in order to produce knowledge? To my understanding, they never came up with it. The debate largely degenerated into a series of longer and longer sets of conditions attached to the traditional one alongside more and more arcane examples to show in each case why that particular proposal wouldn't work. Suffice it to say that the entire exercise did not redound to philosophy's greater glory.

My suggestion, which is probably the majority view in philosophy, is this: Why don't we just say that knowledge is justified true belief, *all things being equal,* and leave it to somebody else to figure out what happens in the bizarre cases?

Undoubtedly, there are those who will ask whether this isn't just a dodge. In part, it is. But only in part. What we're interested in here is the role that knowledge plays in our practices and in our lives. And whatever knowledge is, it's got to have something important to do with belief, truth, and justification. So for our purposes, we can leave things where they are, recognize that there is more to the issue of the definition of knowledge than we have covered, and then move on. After all, we can't do everything here. We're philosophers, not magicians. So we'll just say, "That's good enough for now," and grant that good enough isn't always everything. In this case, while it is a cop-out, it also might be a bit of wisdom.

If we take that route, then we have before us three elements of knowledge that need to be understood: belief, truth, and justification. Let me preview a bit and say that I won't spend much time on belief, I'll spend a little more on truth (after the discussion of justification), and I'll spend a lot on justification. The reasons for this should become clear as I go along. I'll turn to belief first, because I can address that one most quickly.

There can, in fact, be philosophical puzzles around belief. For instance, there is the issue of whether a person still believes something that he or she expressed belief in several years ago but that is now contrary to other things he or she believes. For example, suppose that several years ago I believed that my friend was a decent fellow, and even went so far as to tell you that you ought to make his acquaintance because he's such a decent fellow. Recently, I discovered that this friend of mine has abused the trust of several other mutual friends. Now, I've never said to anybody that I don't think of this person as decent any longer; I may not have thought about the issue that much myself. (Perhaps this person was never a close friend.) Would it be right to assume that I no longer believe that this person is a decent fellow, since that seems to contradict other things that I know about him? Or, since it's at least possible that I'm warped enough to think that people who abuse friendships are still decent people, and since I've never officially taken back the first belief, should you assume that I still think this person is a decent fellow? Or, as yet another alternative, should you say that you can't tell what I believe about his decency?

Of course, you can resolve the situation easily enough: you can ask me whether I still believe that this person is a decent fellow. And that kind of solution will work for this case, as long as I'm honest. The problem is that there are too many cases of this kind. People express all sorts of beliefs that may or may not be in conflict with all sorts of things that they come to believe later. So the problem of what can be counted as being believed is, in fact, a live one.

That's not the only problem that might attach to belief, but it does illustrate that we can't assume that the concept of belief is one that we can take for granted as understood. If knowledge has to do with justified true belief, the questions of what is believed and of what constitutes belief are legitimate ones to ask.

Why, then, am I not worried about the concept of belief? Because when I finish elaborating on the concept of justification, that concept will solve as much of the problem of belief as seems to need solving, at least for our purposes. Specifically, it will solve the problem of what, given certain beliefs that I express publicly, I *ought* to believe or *am committed* to believing. Whether I do believe these other things is, from this perspective, a psychological matter more than a philosophical one. To put the point another way, what our philosophical understanding of justification will allow us to see is how belief ought to go. If belief doesn't actually go in that direction, so be it, but that's an issue about which we won't need to worry. We'll assume that people believe what they say they believe and that they ought to believe whatever follows from that. If, in a specific case, there does happen to be a contradiction somewhere between what people believe and what they ought to believe (i.e., what follows from what they actually say they believe), then there is an incoherence that makes belief (and therefore knowledge) difficult to sort out.

If this sounds a bit vague and abstract, it should. It will make more sense after the discussion of justification which, as I noted, is at the heart of my view of knowledge. So let me turn to the issue of justification without any further ado. Except this further ado: I've already mentioned that the account of knowledge that I give here is indebted to the work of Ludwig Wittgenstein. It's also indebted to a contemporary philosopher, Robert Brandom, whose book *Making It Explicit* provides the model for much of what follows. My own writings on the issue of knowledge are largely drawn from this work as well as from my studying with him several years before the appearance of *Making It Explicit*. Brandom, who traces his philosophical lineage back through the philosopher Wilfrid Sellars to Wittgenstein, seems to me to have gone the furthest in working out how it is that knowledge is a matter of practices. And in order to do so, he focuses on justification. This seems to be exactly the right focus, so I'll turn to justification next.

JUSTIFICATION

Justification is a matter of giving (or at least having) reasons for what one believes. If I tell you that natural selection is the best theory for explaining species evolution, or that clitoridectomy is wrong, or that your boss only hired you for your looks, you may well ask me (or, even if you don't ask me, you may well think of asking me), "How do you know?" And asking me how I know is asking me for the justification for my belief, for the reasons or the evidence I have on the basis of which I believe my claim to be true.

It's worth noting that there are some kinds of claims for which we don't usually ask justification (unless we're in some very unusual circumstances). Wittgenstein liked the example of a claim about one's name. If you ask me what my name is, and I say, "It's Todd," we don't usually think it appropriate to ask, "How do you know?" The reason for this is that we don't usually think that claims about our names are the sorts of statements that require reasons. But that's not because we think that people know their names without reasons, or that they have really good reasons for believing that they know their names. Rather, according to Wittgenstein, claims about one's name are not the kind of thing one should be said, strictly, to *know* at all. But the reasons we should not be said to *know* these claims have nothing to do with any skepticism about our names. It's not that since we don't know our names, we somehow *fail* to know them. Instead, the kinds of claims in question here (of which a claim about one's name serves as an example) are claims that form the framework within which issues of knowing and not-knowing are raised. That is to say, it is because we can, in most cases, claim certainty about our names that we can get into questions of knowledge at all. Claims about one's name—and claims like it—are the framework for knowledge, and specific issues of knowledge unfold within that framework. Why this is so should emerge more clearly as the discussion proceeds. For now, let's just keep hold of the point that there are certain claims about which it is generally appropriate to ask, "How do you know?"—and others about which it is not.

(Many of you will notice that I have hedged here, using words like "generally appropriate" and "usually" and "very unusual circumstances." That's because there are some circumstances in which it might actually be appropriate to ask questions about how one knows what one's name is. Take, for instance, the case of the amnesiac who might think, based on a specific recent event, that he or she is beginning to remember his or her identity. In this case, it might be appropriate to ask what the experience was and what about it seemed to foster some sort of recognition. So we shouldn't think that there are certain kinds of claims that are *always* immune to the question, "How do you know?" Rather, the kinds of claims that count as "framework claims" may well shift from situation to situation, although there is probably a certain degree of uniformity involved.)

Let's turn then to the kinds of claims for which the question "How do you know?" *is* appropriate in most cases. And let's use our three sample claims—about natural selection, clitoridectomy, and your boss—as paradigmatic cases of the appropriateness of raising that question. What I want to do as this part of the book progresses is to look at each example and ask what kinds of claims would count as justification or support for believing the claim in question. In other words, I want to look at three case studies of justification in order to get a sense of how justification works. On the basis of each these three case studies, we'll be able to come to some larger and more general conclusions about justification, ones that will help us see the relation between justification and practices.

I hope that many of you find it uncontroversial to say that the overwhelmingly best theory for explaining species change is natural selection. In our country as a whole, natural selection is less popular than creationism. But I'm guessing that our country as a whole is unlikely to read this book. So, let's suppose that, like me, you think that natural selection beats the "theory" of creationism. And let's further suppose that you met a creationist, one who asked you to justify your belief in natural selection over creationism. What might you reply?

Here are several suggestions, all of which might have already occurred to you. First, the fossil record seems to date back a good long time and shows different species at different times. Unless God kept changing Her mind about species, creationism would seem to be a bad explanatory strategy for the fossil record. Second, molecular genetics seems to point pretty clearly toward natural selection and away from creationism. One can explain the differences in species by analyzing the genetic mutations that persist over time as animals adapt to their environment (and can do so without having to resort to theological intervention). Third, we have contemporary evidence that, as environmental conditions change, certain species become threatened. Witness, for example, the spotted owl in the Northwest or the extinction of the dodo.

These, I know, are pretty superficial reasons that need to be fleshed out more to make the case for natural selection. I won't do that here, since that would take us too far afield of the point of the example. Even with this superficial approach, however, you can see that there is something that connects all of these justifications: they are all justifications that are either biological or closely linked to biology. The first reason, actually, is paleontological, referring to the fossil record. But biology is closely linked to paleontology, which often serves as a history of biological species. The other two reasons are fairly straightforwardly biological.

So what's the point here? The reasons or justifications that we give when we are confronted with questions about biology come, in fact, from *within* the practice of biology or from within practices that intersect with it (e.g., paleontology). This observation should not be surprising, although the consequences of recognizing it might be. The reason it should not be surprising is that when one wants to answer a biological question, the most obvious place to look is to other biological findings that might offer us the answer to that question. But there is a deeper reason as well. The kinds of things that count as decent answers to biological questions are partly *determined* or at least *circumscribed* by the state of biological science—and the state of those sciences that intersect with it—at a given moment. And in the case of this particular biological question, an answer that denies central tenets of molecular genetics or paleontology will not get off the ground with most folks who are familiar with those areas.

Why won't it?

Because you have to start somewhere, and where better to start than with other things that you already think you know? Let me explain.

If we are evaluating several possible answers to a given question, we must have some criteria by which to evaluate them. (Otherwise, we're just throwing up our hands, as, for instance, some—but by no means all—multiculturalists do when they say that any perspective is just as good as any other perspective.) And one of the most important criteria for evaluating such answers is the degree to which a proposed answer converges with what is currently accepted. In the case at hand— natural selection versus creationism—what is currently accepted are certain theories and findings around species change, molecular genetics, and so on. Natural selection converges with these currently accepted theories much better than creationism does (indeed, in some of its incarnations, creationism has to deny them all wholesale). So natural selection is, on this criterion at least, a better theory.

Some of you will already be able to see where this is leading: one of the central criteria for a good theoretical proposal in biology is that of fit with the accepted theories and findings in the current state of the practice of biology. Or, to put the point in another way, the current state of the practice of biology is going to be largely determinative of what counts as a justification for accepting a proposal in biology.

The larger idea that I'm beginning to push here, in a very preliminary way, is that justification is the kind of thing that happens in the context of practices. Giving reasons for what one believes is largely a matter of relying on the connections between what one believes and what is already accepted in the current state of a practice. Now, that isn't the whole story. It can, in fact, get much more complicated. For instance, one could question something that is generally accepted in a given practice on the basis of something that is justifiable on the basis of a *different* practice. I'll turn to issues like that in a bit. (And, if what we get to still isn't enough, then let me recommend Joseph Rouse's *Engaging Science* as a thorough development of a practice-oriented approach to science.) I want to keep things as simple as possible, though, for the moment, so that I don't lose the focus on the core idea. So for now let me underscore the point that giving reasons in the debate over natural selection and creationism has largely to do with justifying a belief in natural selection by referring to other theories, themselves justified, that are part of the current state of the practice of biology.

Faced with what I have said so far in the example of natural selection, there are at least three kinds of questions one might have. First, one might ask whether all justification for preferring natural selection must refer to the practice of biology. Certainly this does not seem to be the case, even in the example I used. There, I referred to other practices (e.g., paleontology) as well. Second, one might ask about what happens when you have a finding (as opposed to a general theory) that doesn't converge with currently accepted theories and findings. In other words, what happens when you have anomalous findings? In the history of science, it is often the anomalous finding that helps provoke the most profound theoretical changes—and it might seem that the view I'm promoting here dismisses that possibility out of hand, since it appears to require everything to fit into currently accepted theories and findings. Third, why can't someone just reject current practices altogether? Isn't that at least a logical possibility?

Let me examine each of these three sets of questions in turn. This will take a little while, but when we're finished, we'll have a pretty good picture of justification and its relation to practices—one that we can use to analyze the examples of clitoridectomy and your boss.

JUSTIFICATION WITHIN AND ACROSS PRACTICES

First let's turn to the issue of justifying a belief in natural selection by reference to practices outside biology. There certainly seems to be no problem with this. It's not as though people have only one practice in which they're engaged, or as though only justifications that fit within the context of that practice will do. In fact, the situation is very different from that. You can look at your own life for examples. Certain kinds of justifications work in your career, others work in your home life, still others work given your political perspective, and so on. The different kinds of practices in which we're involved help determine the kinds of things that we will accept as justifications for beliefs that we (or others) may have.

Now, given that we are all involved in different practices, there is the possibility of certain kinds of contradictions among our beliefs. We might discover, for instance, that we are willing to endorse a claim that can be justified in one practice and, *at the same time,* that we are just as willing to endorse a contradictory claim that is justified in a different practice in which we also participate. Often, becoming aware of a situation like that causes a personal crisis. Think, for instance, of the guy who works at the kind of job in which lying is considered justifiable on the grounds that the most important thing to do in this kind of job is to get ahead of the next guy. (Okay, many of you are

thinking about lawyers. As a professor, academics leap to my mind.)
But suppose that this guy is trying, at home, to teach his kids integrity.
And suppose that one of the kids, growing older, catches on and asks
his father one evening over dinner, "Dad, how come you talk about
integrity so much but don't seem to practice it at work?" You see the
problem here. What is justified in the course of one practice might
not be justified in another, and inasmuch as this guy embraces *both*
practices, he's living a conflict.

When faced with conflicts such as these, we often try to change
one or another of our commitments in order to defuse the conflict.
This guy, for example, could try to have more integrity at work or
change his views on integrity. Or, if he likes weaseling, he could try
to explain how the lesson of integrity he's been teaching all along
must be applied judiciously. But however he approaches it, he'll try to
get out of the conflict.

Science is like that, only more so. It tries to achieve a consistent fit
not only within its individual practices (biology, physics, chemistry,
and the like) but also across practices. That is to say that theories in
biology, for instance, try to converge with theories and findings in
physics, chemistry, and elsewhere. Scientists strive not only for *internal*
fit among the theories and findings in a given field but also for *external*
fit among their theories and findings and those theories and findings of
other sciences. Or, to put the matter in terms of practices and justification, scientists seek to justify their theories not only within their
specific practices but also within the practices of other sciences as well.
That's part of what gives science its unified character as well as its
rigor.

Turning back to the first question we raised—that of justification
outside of one's practice—there seems to be no problem with doing
that while still holding on to the idea that justification is a matter of
practices. We have seen two examples of justification outside of a
single practice—the guy trying to teach integrity to his son and the
biological justifications for natural selection. In the case of the guy, the
justification involved the practices of his work and his home life. In
the case of biology, the justification is both within biology and within
the sciences with which biology wants to converge. The point to
keep in mind here is that although justification can occur with refer-

ence to more than one practice, it never requires us to step *outside practices altogether*. When we seek or give reasons for what we believe, we always do so within the context of some practice or another, even when we find ourselves in the more complicated situation of trying to justify ourselves within the context of two or more practices at the same time.

Let me introduce a term here, and then I'll use it to help sketch out a picture of justification. The term is *inference*. Inference is a move in reasoning. It's often a move from a premise to a necessary conclusion, but it doesn't have to be like that. For instance, just as one can move from the two premises "All men are mortal" and "Socrates is a man" to the conclusion that "Socrates is mortal," one can also move from the claim "The Yankees have the best record in baseball" to the claim "The Yankees have a good chance of winning the World Series this year." The example of Socrates involves a logical inference. The second example is one that works not so much by traditional logic as by knowing one's way around the practice of baseball a bit. So an inference, if we want to define it, is a move from a claim or set of claims to another claim or set of claims for which the first claim or set of claims is supposed to provide support.

Offering justification in the context of practices is an inferential activity. There are certain claims or sets of claims—in the example of natural selection that we are currently investigating, they are the contemporary theories and findings in various sciences—that form the supporting network for other claims. These claims or sets of claims also offer the criteria by which to evaluate competing claims. Justifying a belief amounts to making inferential moves from claims for which the justification seems more secure to the belief one is trying to justify. Depending on the kind of justification one is doing, a belief will be justified by reference to a single set of claims—the claims of one practice—or by reference to several sets of claims at once—the claims of several practices. In the case at hand, we can justify our belief in natural selection by inferring that natural selection is what one would expect, given some less controversial claims *within* biology about molecular genetics, and as well *outside* of biology, in practices like paleontology and so forth.

What I have said so far about justification implies that practices are,

among other things, also webs of inferential relations. That is to say
that practices involve whole networks of inferences that are related to
one another. In psychoanalysis, for example, the claim that a client
transfers his internal conflicts with his parents to the therapist is related
to a whole series of other claims about the nature of people's histories
and emotional lives. Those claims are part of what one commits to in
the course of engaging in the practice of psychoanalysis. Or, to return
to an earlier example, if one is engaged in Chinese cooking one can
infer from the claim "The snow peas have been simmering for ten
minutes" the conclusion "The snow peas are overcooked." This is an
inference that cannot be made in other cooking practices—and was
certainly never made in the home in which I grew up—but it can be
made in Chinese cooking.

The importance of the idea of practices as involving networks of
inferential relations lies in the picture it gives us of how justification,
and thus knowledge, works. Think for a moment of how different
this picture is from the foundationalist picture of justification. For the
foundationalist, there are certain indubitable claims that form the bedrock for all attempts at justification. In the view I am putting forward
here, justification happens within the context of practices (or groups
of practices) that provide all the bedrock there is for justification.
There is nothing to justify the practices themselves, except perhaps
other practices which are equally unsupported. In the end, then, when
one takes a practice-oriented view of knowledge, one loses the idea
that there can be any kind of ultimate support for our knowledge, and
foundationalism comes to seem misguided.

One might well be tempted to ask here whether engaging in a
practice requires that one accept all of the claims of that practice. That
question, in fact, is closely related to the second of the three questions
I raised earlier: What happens in science when you have anomalous
findings? Before trying to answer it, we should probably pause on the
path we've just followed in order to get an overview of where it has
led us. We started with the question of whether justification happens
across practices and not merely within them. The answer was *yes*.
Practices involve networks of inferential relations, and those inferential relations are often themselves inferentially related to other practices and their networks of justification—as in science. Therefore,

justifying is a matter of engaging in inferential activity within and across the context of practices. Or, to put the point in another way, justifying is a matter of giving reasons for what one believes that are acceptable within the context of the inferential relations that hold in one or more practices.

In answering the question of justification across as well as within practices, I momentarily assumed that the network of inferential relations in a given practice or practices was fixed. In other words, I assumed that the relationships between claims formed some kind of stable, static whole. But anybody who knows anything about science—or for that matter, about any other kind of knowledge—recognizes that things aren't at all like that. The kinds of claims endorsed within a particular practice change all the time. And since claims are inferentially related to one another—some claims supporting others in certain ways, others being supported in certain ways—as the kinds of claims that are endorsed change, so does the inferential network of the practice. (Think here of that old game Twister, in which people stretch themselves in various ways in order to touch designated brightly colored patches on a mat. As new colors are called out, or as people come and go from the game, others have to rearrange their positions so that they don't collapse on one another. In a practice, claims do much the same thing. As new claims are brought into the practice or old claims become discredited, the inferential relations among the remaining claims are, to a greater or lesser extent, rearranged.)

So what happens when an anomalous finding occurs in science? Well, the first thing that happens is that most people engaged in the practice try to deny it. After all, they're already committed to claims that are opposed to this particular finding (or else it wouldn't be anomalous). But suppose the anomalous finding has staying power: it keeps coming up in repeated experiments, more people come to believe that it is true, things like that. Then some kind of change in the practice has to occur. However, where that change must occur isn't necessarily given. To see why not, let me give a semi-historical example.

Suppose there was a society that permitted slavery, a society in which the slaveowners justified the keeping of slaves by the claim that people of a skin color different from their own were not fully human and were thus subject to being harnessed for work in much the same way that other beasts of burden are. Now, as this society evolves, the slaves give every evidence of being like the slaveowners in abilities such as intelligence, emotional expression, and the like. At first, the slaveowners would be tempted to deny the likeness. But suppose it persists to the point at which there seems to be something terribly unjust about slavery. Now there has to be a change in people's thinking about slavery. The anomalous finding—that slaves are more like slaveowners than previously thought—has to be accommodated somehow. But how? In fact, there are several ways in which the accommodation could occur. One way would be to recognize that slaves are fully human and to free them. But that isn't the only way. Another way to accommodate the anomalous finding would be to say that slaves are more like humans than previously thought and that therefore their conditions of slavery should be made easier. Or, one could argue that slaves are demonic representations of humans provided by an evil deity and that they should all be killed. Given the other practices in which the people in this society are engaged and the claims endorsed by those other practices, one or another of these options might seem more likely. But no *particular* option is *necessarily* required to solve the problem of the anomaly. Something must change, but what it is that must change is open to discussion, debate, and also some strategizing.

The idea that changes that occur in practices don't necessarily have to occur at a single point leads us to another important aspect of justification in practices (one on which the philosopher Wilfrid Sellars was particularly keen). In a practice, no particular generally accepted claim or theory is immune to criticism. One can, if one has the proper evidence, raise doubts about any claim in the practice. And, given what we've just seen, one can often raise doubts at one or more of several different places. What one *can't* do, as long as one endorses or participates in the practice, is question all of the claims and theories at the same time. If one did that, one would no longer be participating in the practice.

To see why, let's look at another example. Suppose one were to assess the psychoanalytic claim that clients transfer their familial con-

flicts to the analyst. Now suppose further that evidence arose suggest-
ing that the kinds of talk and behavior that would be expected if
clients *did* transfer those conflicts to the analyst never really material-
ized. Well, that might bring some people to doubt the claim that
clients really do transfer the familial conflicts in the way suggested by
psychoanalysts. But, as we've just seen, one doesn't have to doubt that
particular claim. One could, for instance, continue to believe that
clients do transfer their feelings to the therapist, but that they do so
unconsciously. In that case, given the other claims supporting the
practice of psychoanalysis, one might have to give up the idea that
working through the transference is a proper approach to therapy. But
that is different from giving up the idea that there is any transference.

But suppose that one goes even further than this. Suppose that one
begins to doubt that there is transference, and (therefore) to doubt that
working through the transference is a proper approach to therapy.
And suppose that the reason for doubting those claims is that it seems
increasingly unlikely that there is such a thing as an unconscious, in
the psychoanalytic sense, and (therefore) that there is such a thing as
repression. And—why not go the whole hog here?—suppose that one
doubts that familial conflicts play a particularly important develop-
mental role in who one ultimately becomes. Well. In that case, we are
no longer rethinking the practice of psychoanalysis; we are abandoning it. (This is precisely the recommendation of some recent critics
of psychoanalysis, who doubt most of the fundamental concepts to
which that practice is committed.)

Let me spend a moment summing up the previous few pages, and
then turn back to the issue of natural selection. What I have been
arguing here is that the idea that people are committed to the claims,
findings, theories, and so on of a particular practice does not mean
that they are committed to *all* of them. Nor do they have to be. They
may be committed to some and not to others. Moreover, there is no
particular claim or theory or finding in a given practice that is necessarily immune from criticism or change. You can criticize certain
claims in a practice on the basis of others in that practice or in related
practices. To be committed to a practice, then, is to be committed to
enough of the claims, findings, and theories of that practice—and
particularly its "central" claims, findings, theories, and so on—as to be

reasonably seen as being committed to it. (We might think of the difference between a practice's "central" claims and its "non-central" ones as the difference between those claims that are usually used to justify other claims and those claims that are usually on the receiving end of justification. The central claims would be the ones that I noted at the beginning of this part of the book—the ones Wittgenstein said that we wouldn't know how to justify except in certain unusual circumstances. They are the claims that we don't, strictly speaking, know; instead, they help set the framework for asking about which claims we know and don't know. But, as we will see, even the central claims can come up for scrutiny.)

All of this is important in understanding how justification works within the context of practices. How, specifically, does it apply to natural selection?

We have already seen, in answering the first question raised by my account of the relation of justification to practices, that one can justify natural selection by reference not only to the practice of biology but also to other related practices. But the second question expressed the worry that practices are static wholes that are resistant to change. The creationist here might want to argue that there is something circular about using biology to defend natural selection, since some of the biological findings themselves could be wrong. In my view, the proper answer to this response is, "Yes, they could be." But recognizing the potential mistakenness of certain claims, findings, or theories is just part of the framework of science. We should not think of scientific practices (or of most other practices) as static groups of claims that are inferentially interlocked into an unchangeable whole. Rather, we should think of them as ongoing social activities that involve networks of claims that are more or less closely inferentially related. Thinking of practices in this way helps us see how practices have a holistic aspect: they are tied together by their goals, by the people participating in them, and by the inferential connections among their claims and theories. At the same time, though, they are dynamic, evolving wholes, not rigid ones.

So the believer in natural selection might reply to the creationist who says that biology might have findings or theories or claims that are mistaken, "Yes, but which ones? And how do they affect natural selection as an account of species change?" There, the creationist might find himself or herself at a loss. Since science tends to be a self-correcting activity, the mere act of challenging biological claims won't work. One needs to give a reason for challenging them. And most scientists already do that when it seems appropriate. So it isn't enough to issue some kind of bare challenge when confronted with the scientific evidence for natural selection. We can't, as many kids do, just say "How do you know?" What we must do, if we're going to be intellectually honest about it, is to take up the practice and challenge some claims or theories or findings or whatever on the basis of others. (As we'll see in a bit, there's another type of legitimate challenge one can make, but it involves another story.) When we go that route, life becomes increasingly difficult for the creationist.

But might the creationist have another move altogether? Might he or she make a more wholesale challenge, such as the one we imagined as a critique of psychoanalysis? Might he or she just reject biology, paleontology, and so on as practices, and simply stand in favor of creationism? Isn't that at least a coherent move, if not a particularly desirable one?

This move, in fact, is what emerges in the third question we raised earlier: the logical possibility of rejecting certain practices altogether. Now, it seems to me that such wholesale rejection can occur on at least two grounds, the second ground more legitimate than the first (although, as we'll notice, the distinction between these two grounds is not as clear-cut as it might be). The first ground for rejecting the whole set of claims in a practice is that the practice's perspective just doesn't fit one's particular beliefs at a particular time. That is probably the point at which many creationists find themselves when confronted with scientific evidence in favor of natural selection. The other, more legitimate rejection would happen for more legitimate reasons—reasons that originate in another practice one endorses. Let me look at each in turn.

What the creationist can do, and there are certainly plenty who seem to do it, is reject the practices of biology and other scientific fields outright, since they seem to conflict with the claims the creationist wants to hold. There is nothing incoherent about this. In fact, the reason some creationists want to engage in such a wholesale rejection is precisely *in order* to maintain the coherence of their creationist viewpoint. Their reasoning, to put the matter in a nutshell, goes something like this: Since scientific practices and creationism are not logically compatible, and since I want to be a creationist who isn't illogical, I'll reject any scientific practice that conflicts with creationism.

This seems to me to be a position one can take. In fact, when we talk about the beliefs of very different cultures later in this part of the book, I'll argue that this kind of position may be the only one available. And for the creationist, it does have the advantage that you can't argue with it, since everything you're going to bring forward as evidence against creationism has already been rejected before the discussion starts. My response to this position is not to offer a reasoned response—since I don't share enough with this type of creationist to engage in reasoning with him or her—but just to try to make sure that he or she doesn't wind up teaching one of my kids.

It is worth noting in passing the structural similarity of this position to that of another position that sometimes floats around philosophical circles. I'll call it the position of the "coherent Nazi." Is it possible, one might ask, coherently to be a Nazi? Well, if one lines up all of one's beliefs in the right way, it is. To be a Nazi in the sense of someone committed to the destruction of Jews, one would have to believe, for instance, that Jews aren't the moral equal of non-Jews, that they are an evil force, and that it is morally okay to eradicate evil forces that are not the moral equivalent of non-Jews. This puts the picture a bit simply, but we can see how it works. Now suppose one were to try to argue against the Nazi about the first claim, that Jews are not the moral equal of non-Jews. One might point out the diversity of Jewish lives, show how that diversity reflects a diversity in the lives of non-Jews, and generally raise questions about the propriety of ascribing this moral inferiority to an entire group. You could do this. But the Nazi could hold firm here, and say that there is something in Jewish culture that lends itself to moral inferiority. Even though that moral inferiority can't be glimpsed in every Jew, nevertheless it is a Jewish trait that will come out sooner or later, and thus it taints every Jew. Well, this could keep going, and the position of the Nazi could become harder and harder to defend, requiring the Nazi to abandon any number of reasonable beliefs and embrace any number of really weird ones. But there remains the possibility of being coherent, if the Nazi would be willing to give up enough other reasonable beliefs in order to do it. I don't see how Nazism, then, is *necessarily* incoherent. It's wrong, of course. And of course most Nazis themselves, if pressed, would surely wind up being incoherent. But if one is willing to give up enough in the way of other beliefs in order to defend Nazism (or, alternatively, hold enough in the way of wild beliefs in order to defend it), then the position will at least remain coherent, in the minimal sense that the Nazi's beliefs are logically compatible with one another. In other words, one can be a Nazi, and even a coherent (if barbaric) one, by more or less dismissing all of the evidence that conflicts with one's Nazi beliefs.

So far, we've been looking at the possibility of rejecting entire practices and their claims and theories just because one doesn't like them. I've argued that such a rejection is coherent, if not particularly palatable. There is another (and to my mind better-motivated) way to attack a practice, however: by referring to an uncontroversial practice whose claims are incompatible with the claims of the rejected practice. In this case, one might reject a practice for reasons that are good reasons, assuming that one embraces the practice on the basis of which the first practice is rejected. (The idea that it is uncontroversial would imply that one could generally expect that others embrace it.)

As an example, let's return to the practice of psychoanalysis. Psychoanalysis is a good example of a practice, since it has its own goals, norms, and regularities; moreover, those goals, norms, and regularities are still fairly distinct from those of mainstream psychology (although there are some overlaps). Now suppose, as I supposed earlier, that one were to criticize psychoanalysis as an entire practice, as opposed to criticizing a particular claim or theory within psychoanalysis. How might one do it?

One way is through the practice of philosophy, and particularly that branch of philosophy known as philosophy of science. One of the tasks of philosophy of science is to discover or propose criteria for distinguishing good science from bad science. Different proposals have been discussed over the years, but among the criteria for a good science (or a good theory within a particular science) are its ability to explain, its testability, its simplicity, and its convergence with other known scientific theories and findings. Now many people have claimed that psychoanalysis fails to meet at least two of these criteria: testability and convergence with other known scientific theories and findings. I don't want to argue about the truth of that claim. Rather, my point is that *if* psychoanalysis failed to meet those criteria—as defined by philosophers of science—then people who embraced philosophy of science would have a reason to reject psychoanalysis as a practice. It would be incompatible with beliefs they held about what constitutes a good science. In this case—as opposed to the case in which one rejects a practice just because one doesn't like its claims—we have a better-motivated rejection of an entire practice.

I can imagine at this point a strong objection coming from some readers to the distinction I have made between better- and worse-motivated reasons for rejecting a practice. Couldn't one say to me here that there is no real distinction between the case of the creationist rejecting large swaths of science and the case of the philosopher of science rejecting psychoanalysis? After all, in both cases a practice is rejected on the basis of another practice whose claims, theories, and so on are incompatible with it. What would be the distinction between the two cases?

Frankly, this is a very good objection.

I have to concede here that there is the kind of deep link between the two cases that the objection states. In both cases, a practice is rejected based upon its incompatibility (in terms of knowledge) with another practice. But I'm not prepared to go so far as to say that the two rejections are *equally* strongly motivated. The distinction that I want to maintain rests not so much upon the rejection of one practice in favor of another as it does upon which practices we can expect fellow members of our society to embrace in deciding between better and worse practices. (By better and worse here, I mean better and worse relative to the issue at hand, that of knowledge.) In the first case, what must be rejected in order to maintain creationism is so broad and deep and so tightly linked with other beliefs (including those based on simple observation) that the rejection looks more like an attempt to hold on to something than to get at the truth of the matter. In the case of psychoanalysis, the situation is nearly reversed.

The criteria for a good science, based upon study of many other well-developed sciences, are broad and deep and reflect something important about what constitutes a good scientific practice. If it turns out that psychoanalysis violates those criteria, there would indeed be good reason to reject psychoanalysis.

(This, by the way, is the character of the "faith" in science I referred to earlier in discussing the illusion of metaphysical depth.)

In order to defend my position here, I would have to go further afield than would be helpful in a book about practices, although I'll return to this issue a bit in the discussion of clitoridectomy. So, rather than try to compel assent, let me say that if what I've just argued is not convincing, it doesn't change anything of consequence. For the purposes of my account, I don't need to persuade you that there is a significant difference between the creationist rejecting science and the hypothetical philosopher of science rejecting psychoanalysis. As long as you're prepared to accept that the rejection of the claims to knowledge of an entire practice cannot happen for reasons outside of or beyond all practices—except, I guess, for pure caprice—then we've agreed on the important point.

Let me spend a moment giving a quick overview of where we've just been. In this section, I've spent a lot of time trying to deepen the account of knowledge within practices by considering three questions that arose in the treatment of justifying natural selection over creationism. These questions had to do with justification across practices, justification within practices, and the justification of the rejection of a particular practice altogether. Throughout this discussion, I have not referred to certain beliefs that *must* be embraced, period. The view that there are certain beliefs that *must* be embraced, period, is foundationalism. If one takes a view of knowledge as a matter of practices, then what must or must not be believed is related to what practices one does or does not embrace. Moreover, the embrace of one practice or another is always a bit arbitrary, in the specific sense that nothing (except perhaps another practice) guarantees that it is, from the standpoint of knowledge, the *right* practice to embrace. That kind of arbitrariness is necessary to any account of knowledge that is not foundationalist, since any nonfoundationalist account of knowledge must be characterized by a lack of epistemic guarantees (that is, knowledge-based guarantees). What foundationalism tried to offer us was a way in which to guarantee that certain claims to knowledge were right, regardless of the practices in which we were engaged or whose claims we happened to embrace. With the failure of foundationalism, we must live with the fact that our knowledge has no ultimate guarantee.

This does not imply that knowledge claims are *completely* arbitrary. We can often give reasons for what we believe. What it does imply is that sooner or later those reasons run out, and we wind up saying something like, "If you don't believe that, we might as well end this discussion." Or, as Wittgenstein put it, "This is how I act." When you run out of reasons in a particular practice, you might try to defend it by defending the approach to knowledge of the whole practice. But even then, the reasons you give for defending that approach will come from the vantage point of another practice, whose reasons sooner or later will run out. When it comes to knowledge, there simply are no cosmic guarantees.

CLITORIDECTOMY

We have looked at length at the example of justifying a belief in natural selection, because it has allowed us to get an entire overview of how justification looks when you recognize that it is a matter of practices. Starting with a scientific example has also added some simplicity for us, since the web of scientific belief is fairly tightly drawn among the various scientific practices. The next example, that of clitoridectomy, will draw us into a more tangled web. Since it involves moral issues, clitoridectomy will bring in certain complexities that do not appear in the natural selection example. However, nothing I've said in the natural selection example will change when we discuss clitoridectomy or analyze the claim that your boss only hired you for your looks. It sets the basic structure that we can work from in the cases to which I now want to turn.

The first of these cases will be the justification for the claim, "Clitoridectomy is morally wrong." In this example, we have moved from a scientific claim to a moral one. But we still have an issue of knowledge on our hands. We have a belief, one for which we are seeking justification, and if that justification is forthcoming, we may hold the belief to be true. Justified true belief: knowledge. Now there may be people who will want to say something like, "Wait a minute. Science is a matter of knowledge, but morality is just about people's personal views." I would argue that that's mistaken, but it will take the analysis of this example to give that argument some plausibility. What I hope to be convincing about here is that morality and science both involve issues of knowledge. There is, certainly, a deep difference between them, but that difference doesn't run along the fault line that divides knowledge from opinion.

So what might be the justification for thinking that clitoridectomy is wrong? Someone might offer several reasons. First, it reduces a woman's sexual pleasure. Second, it's often dangerous, and can have fatal complications. Third, the fact that it removes a woman's organ of pleasure but not a man's makes it an act of oppression against women. Let's stick with those, since we really don't need any more.

The first thing to notice here is that we are working with inferences, just as we worked with inferences when we discussed natural selection. Here we have some claims that we may want to hold about the effects of clitoridectomy and the moral wrongness of those effects, and on the basis of those claims we infer the moral wrongness of clitoridectomy. One claim that we might hold, for instance, is that oppression against women is morally wrong. From that, we could infer that inasmuch as clitoridectomy is a form of oppression against women, it too is morally wrong. However, we might even go a step further, at least linguistically, and say that the claim "Oppression against women is morally wrong" is already redundant. That is, since we can infer from something's being oppressive that it is morally wrong, once we say it's oppressive we don't need to create that extra link in our inferential chain.

That latter move is probably right. Something's being oppressive does seem to make it immediately morally wrong. We know this because in the practice of moral theorizing, the acceptance that something is oppressive counts as a moral strike against it. That does not mean that something's being oppressive means, in all cases, that we should not do it. It might turn out, for instance, that all of our options are oppressive, and so we are forced to pick the least oppressive one. But oppression certainly does count immediately as a moral strike against whatever it is that we are calling oppressive.

You might have noticed that I called the practice in which the word "oppressive" is used "moral theorizing" rather than "morality." That wasn't an accident. The way I see things (and I'll defend this some more at the beginning of the next chapter), morality appears in many practices. However, when one begins, often within the context of a particular practice, to reflect on the moral rightness or wrongness of what one is doing, then one usually slips fairly rapidly into the practice of moral theorizing. Moral theorizing, then, is a practice that intersects with lots of other practices, and does so at the moment one becomes philosophically reflective about the moral rightness or wrongness of what one is doing in a particular practice. More on this later.

For right now, the point I want to press is that if we are engaged in the practice of moral theorizing, then one of the inferential moves most of us would be willing to make is from something's being oppressive to its being morally wrong. So, in the case of clitoridectomy, we would infer from its oppressiveness to its wrongness. We would also make that inference from the first two reasons I offered against clitoridectomy—its reducing the sexual pleasure of women and its being dangerous and having often fatal complications. And if this were the end of the matter, then we could immediately conclude that clitoridectomy is morally wrong, and might further conclude that we should discourage it in cultures that practice it.

Of course, this isn't the end of the matter. And the reason it isn't will teach us some lessons both about the difference between morality and science and about the relativity of morality to different cultures. In order to avoid confusion, I want to take these lessons separately. And in order to see the first one, let me suggest a reason why people might think that clitoridectomy is *not* morally wrong.

Some people might argue that clitoridectomy is a necessary aspect of certain cultures, so necessary that those cultures would perish if clitoridectomy were no longer performed. And, inasmuch as the preservation of a diversity of cultures is a good thing, then the necessity of clitoridectomy to a culture's preservation would constitute a reason in favor of it—or a reason against condemning it, at least in some cases. Admittedly this argument is a bit speculative; it's often difficult to tell which practices are necessary aspects of a given culture and which could be given up without profound cultural change occurring. But let's accept it for the moment, at least as an example of what someone might argue in defense of clitoridectomy.

Now there are several ways in which one might attack this argument. One way would be to make the (at least equally speculative) claim that even if clitoridectomy destroyed the current workings of a particular culture, the new culture that would arise in its place might be better than the old one. Another line of attack could be to say that, even though cultural diversity is a good thing, clitoridectomy is such an egregiously immoral practice that cultures engaged in it should not receive protection under the "preservation of cultural diversity" banner. There could be other lines of attack as well. These, however, are enough to illustrate an important difference between science and moral theorizing.

In the back and forth between attacks upon and defenses of clitoridectomy, we have introduced several moral claims on which it is difficult to get agreement. In trying to get that agreement, there are a number of questions we would have to confront. Is cultural diversity a good thing? If so, what kinds of cultural diversity should we support? How do we weigh the moral claims of women to safety and autonomy against the claims of cultural integrity? Is cultural diversity in the current world—under the hegemony of Western consumerism—more important than it was in earlier times? These questions, and doubtless others you have already thought of, are questions that are difficult to answer, in part because it is difficult to get agreement on how we would go about answering them.

In this way, moral questions—and normative questions generally, questions about how we ought to go about doing things—differ significantly from scientific ones. In science, there is an agreed-upon procedure for answering questions: the scientific method of experimentation. That agreed-upon method, in turn, has yielded a body of knowledge that (always pending further experimentation) has received general assent, at least among the scientifically literate. In discussing morality or other normative matters, there is no agreed-upon method for answering the questions that arise. As a result, the body of knowledge that forms the background for asking questions is thinner, more amorphous, and not as tightly woven together as it is in science. That's not to say that there is no background of knowledge in moral matters. For instance, we would all agree that torturing babies just for fun is morally reprehensible, or that people ought to treat one another with a certain degree of respect. But the kinds of background knowledge that we have are more loosely connected, inferentially: the kinds of inferences that we can make from some of the background knowledge, and the claims on which we can really count for knowledge, are not nearly as clearly defined as they are in science. (In the next part of the book, I'll suggest one of the reasons for this looseness of inferential connection.)

We can see this lack of inferential coherence exemplified in such moral debates as abortion. It would be a mistake to think that pro-choice and pro-life advocates have no areas of moral agreement. They agree, for instance, that people have rights and that those rights should be governmentally protected. That agreement isn't enough to bring the two sides together, however. For example, one thing they *don't* agree on is which beings should be counted as people. The reason pro-choice and pro-life advocates can talk to each other at all—even though they often do so in fairly loud voices—is that there is a shared moral background to the debate. That shared moral background may be a thin one, but it does exist.

Before turning to a second line of defense for clitoridectomy, I want to draw two lessons from what we have just seen. The first is that a major distinction—perhaps *the* major distinction—between scientific knowledge and moral knowledge lies in the agreed-upon method in the former that the latter lacks, a method that results in an inferentially tight body of scientific knowledge and a looser body of moral knowledge. The second lesson is that although these distinctions exist, they are not enough to allow us to say that science gives us knowledge but morality only gives us opinion. In both cases, we have belief. In both cases, we have justification: reasons for the belief. And, as we will see below, at least on a certain plausible view of truth, we might equally ascribe truth to the claims in both. Therefore, it seems to me, there is no reason not to speak of moral knowledge, just as we speak of scientific knowledge. Once we get past the idea that any knowledge can have ultimately indubitable foundations and begin to think of it as largely a matter of justification, and then begin to see justification as a matter of being able to give reasons in the context of a practice (or across practices), then the term *knowledge* seems equally applicable to science and morality.

So far, we have been considering a particular way of trying to defend the idea that clitoridectomy may not be morally wrong, arguing that in fact there might be reasons within the context of our broad practice of moral theorizing that would weigh in favor of its moral acceptability. There is another way we might defend clitoridectomy, however. This second way is, ultimately, incoherent. But many people, including certain people who think of themselves as multiculturalists, do in fact hold this view, so it might be worth considering for a moment. In addition, learning why this view fails to cohere will reveal an important truth about our own moral views.

The defense of clitoridectomy that is ultimately incoherent does not work by challenging some of our moral reasons against clitoridectomy with some other reasons in favor of it. Instead, it works by rejecting our moral framework altogether. Put in its most straightforward terms, the argument goes something like this: "People who engage in clitoridectomy are coming from a radically different moral framework from the one that you—the critic of clitoridectomy—inhabit. How do you know that your moral framework is better than theirs is? And if you don't know that your moral framework is better than theirs is, how can you impose your moral framework on them? You have no business imposing a moral framework on others whose moral framework differs from yours."

The first thing to notice about this view is that it works by counterposing moral frameworks rather than by posing moral reason against moral reason. Cast in terms of practices, we might say that the opposition here is between two radically different practices rather than between two justifications that conflict within the context of more or less the same practice. This, you can see right away, is a very different approach to the issue of the rightness or wrongness of clitoridectomy.

Instead of working by giving reasons within the context of a practice, it works by questioning the practice altogether.

This kind of move is not rare. I have read many articles and been to any number of conferences in which people argue for multiculturalism by saying that since no culture's practices are better than any other culture's practices, we need to respect them all equally and not judge among them.

The idea that motivates this view—that we should try to respect the different cultures of others—is an appealing one. But the argument for it, as it stands, won't work. At least, I'm going to try to convince you of that. The problem is that the argument, in order to be attractive, must appeal to reasons that originate in the very moral practice that it is trying to reject.

To see how, turn back to the argument itself. It starts from two premises. The first premise is that the moral framework of our culture is radically different from that of a culture that engages in clitoridectomy. The second premise is that one can't argue for the superiority of one moral framework over another. From those two premises, the argument infers that we have no business imposing our moral framework on that other culture. What I want to focus on here is the inference, the move from premises to conclusion. Before doing so, though, let me call attention to the fact that the first premise itself is a bit shaky. I'm not so sure that cultures around the world differ so radically in their moral frameworks or practices as the premise seems to suggest. Moreover, if they did, it's not at all clear that we would call the corresponding practice of the other culture a *moral* one. It's not that we would call it an *immoral* one. Rather, what we would probably want to say here is that the other culture has no practice that corresponds to our practice of morality. I think that if we located such a culture, we would find it very hard to understand what its members were up to, since morality plays such an important role in our own culture. But I won't linger over that point.

The point I *do* want to linger over is the inference from premises to conclusion. Why should the fact of another culture's moral framework being radically different from our own—combined with the fact that we can't prove our moral framework to be, ultimately, the right one—imply that we can't impose our own framework on that other culture? Such an inference isn't immediately obvious. There's nothing contradictory, after all, in saying that while the premises are true, there is nothing in them that requires that we refrain from imposing our moral framework on others. There certainly isn't anything in the first premise that requires it. And as far as the second premise goes, even though we can't prove that our moral framework is superior (and, after we give up the project of foundationalism, we *won't* be able to prove that), there's nothing contradictory in saying that we don't know that their moral framework is any good either, so let's just let them battle it out.

If we're going to accept the inference, then, we're going to need some reasons to back it up. And, in fact, there are some reasons that leap to mind, even if they don't settle the case. Perhaps we might say that respecting the differences of others from ourselves means that we ought to refrain, where possible, from imposing our moral framework on others. Perhaps we might say that one shouldn't ask other people to act (or to refrain from acting) in ways in which they have no reason to act (or to refrain from acting). Or again, perhaps we might want to argue that the existence of several moral frameworks in the world is a good thing, because it allows us to recognize that there are alternative ways of seeing the world.

Whether these reasons for not imposing our moral framework on others are actually good reasons is, for my purposes, beside the point. (In the end, I don't think they'll amount to a defense of clitoridectomy.) Rather, the point is that all of them—and any others we might think of—*come from our moral practice.* That is to say, the inference—the inferential move from the premises of (1) radically different moral frameworks and (2) no ultimate proof of the superiority of our own framework to the conclusion of not imposing our moral framework on others—only works, if it does work, from within the context of *our* moral framework. Our moral practice. Yours and mine. Or, to put the point in yet another way, the argument offered in favor of not imposing one's moral framework on others only works if one takes one's own moral framework seriously.

And this undermines the argument itself. In order to have a reason to recognize the legitimacy of the moral framework of the other culture, we must appeal to our own moral framework. We must judge the reasons for the other moral framework's legitimacy in terms of our own. Such judgment is inescapable, because the reasons we would find to recognize or to deny the legitimacy of another culture's moral framework have to come from somewhere. And where do they come from? From our own moral framework or practice. And so we cannot, as the argument I'm rejecting would have us do, refrain from judging the moral framework of another culture or imposing our framework on it by laying aside our own moral framework. We can only do it—if we're doing it for a good reason, or for a reason at any rate—by taking our own moral framework seriously.

We cannot, if we are performing any sort of recognizably moral judgment, escape our own moral framework or moral practice. Even when we are trying to come to terms with a moral framework or moral practice radically different from our own. (By introducing the phrase "coming to terms with," I want to include a range of possibilities—imposing upon, respecting, withholding judgment on, limiting, destroying, and so on.) In short, *moral judgments always come from the context of the practice in which such judgments are made.* This may seem to us to be a strange idea, since we are used to thinking that we can step outside our own moral practice and make judgments about it as a whole. However, once we see that justification is a matter of reasons and that reasons happen in the context of practices, then we must give up the idea that there can be *moral* reasons that are given for or against something outside the context of a specific *moral* practice. Morally—or scientifically, or epistemically in general—there is no "view from nowhere" (a phrase I draw from the philosopher Thomas Nagel) that can anchor our judgments. That is one of the costs (if indeed it is a cost) of moving from a foundationalist picture of knowledge to a practice-oriented one.

At this point, someone might be tempted to ask, "If we can't judge a moral theoretical practice from the outside, how can we ever change or develop the judgments made from within the current state of our moral practice?" We do it in much the same way as we do it in scientific practices. When we looked at the issue of natural selection, we saw that scientific practices could change, due to pressure from within the practice or from outside it. Much the same thing happens in moral theoretical practice. We begin to see tensions in holding moral positions that once seemed consistent; a new moral argument leads us to question previous beliefs; a scientific breakthrough turns out to have moral implications. These changes, and many others, allow for development within the context of a moral theoretical practice. To say, then, that moral judgments come inescapably from within the framework of a specific moral practice does not necessarily mean that that practice is immune from change or critique.

Hidden inside the argument I have just made is a response to a charge that has often been leveled at the idea of knowledge occurring in practices: the charge of relativism. I want to spend a bit of time on this charge because it is probably the objection most often raised against the kind of perspective on knowledge that I'm trying to develop. Before responding to the charge, however, it's worth seeing exactly what the objection of relativism is.

There are many forms of *relativism,* which is the idea that a certain set of beliefs, reasons, truths, and the like gain their currency relative to a particular social formation (e.g., culture, society, practice). In the case of practices, to charge the view I'm developing here with relativism would be to make the following sort of argument against it. If I say, "Knowledge is relative to practices," wouldn't that very claim— the claim "Knowledge is relative to practices"—be a claim of knowledge? And if so, wouldn't it also be relative to practices? In other words, wouldn't the claim "Knowledge is relative to practices" be a claim of knowledge only from within the context of certain practices? And wouldn't it hold true, then, only for people who endorse or participate in those certain practices? Moreover, if some people don't accept or endorse those practices from within which I make my claim, wouldn't knowledge *not* be relative for them? In the end, the claim that knowledge is relative to practices is itself a relative claim that only works for some people, those who endorse the particular practices from within which the claim arises. Or, to put the matter another way, the claim that knowledge is relative to practices is not universally true, only relatively true.

This charge, if it's right, is a serious one. The reason it is serious is that I'm trying to push the idea of practices as the centerpiece of any good understanding of knowledge. And, if this objection works, there may be something self-contradictory in my approach. The self-contradiction would be that on the one hand, I want to claim that knowledge is relative to practices, but on the other, I can't do so without the claim itself (the claim "Knowledge is relative to practices") becoming relative, and therefore only partially true. And, since self-contradiction is a good reason to reject a philosophical position, I'd better address this objection.

In addressing it, the first step I want to take is to note that my claim is *not* that knowledge is relative to practices. My claim is that knowledge is inseparable from practices, which is different. Moreover, my claim is not that knowledge—which requires not only justification but also truth and belief—is reducible to practices; when we get to the issue of truth, we'll see how knowledge partly eludes the idea of practices. The idea I *am* trying to defend is that most of the interesting stuff in understanding knowledge is tied up with justification, and that *justification* is relative to practices. So, let me start my response by saying that it is not knowledge but justification that is relative to practices.

But now, is there any problem in saying that justification is relative to practices? No, there isn't. If we are going to try the same relativist move on justification that we just did on knowledge, what we'll have to ask is, Is the claim "Justification is relative to a practice" itself justified relative to a practice? And the answer to that question is *yes*. It is justified relative to a specific practice: the practice of philosophy. And it is that specific practice in which we are engaged right now. In essence, what I have been trying to do in this part of the book is convince you that justification is relative to practices. I have been doing that by giving you justifications—reasons—that are convincing to the extent that you are willing to participate in (or at least endorse) the philosophical practice in which I am engaged. There is nothing self-contradictory about that. If someone rejects the project of philosophy in which I am engaged, he or she may very well not be convinced of what I'm saying. That doesn't mean that what I'm saying is false (falsity has to do with the issue of truth, but here I'm dealing with the issue of justification). It only means that I have not justified myself to that person's satisfaction. Moreover, I will probably not be able to justify myself to his or her satisfaction, because—unless we share some philosophical practice in which to sort all this out—the activity of giving reasons to one another will be futile.

The upshot of this, then, is that the charge of relativism that has been leveled against the perspective I'm developing doesn't work. It rests on a confusion between knowledge as a whole and justification in particular. While the charge of relativism banks on the claim that knowledge is relative to practices, my position is that it is justification—not the entirety of knowledge—that is relative to practices.

We're almost ready to turn to the third sample claim of knowledge that I want to investigate, the claim that your boss only hired you for your looks. But let me spend a moment summarizing this section. In looking at the wrongness of clitoridectomy, we have seen that in some senses, the practice of moral theorizing is similar to many scientific practices. In particular, it involves knowledge, just as science does. In another way, though, the practice of moral theorizing is very different from the practices of science. It lacks science's agreed-upon method, and the inferential connections within moral theorizing (and between moral theorizing and other fields of knowledge) are much looser than they are in science.

Further, we saw that moral theorizing is, in an important way, almost inescapable. In judging other cultures, one cannot abandon one's own moral theoretical practice. This is because the claim that one ought not interfere with a different moral practice is itself justified by the lights of one's *own* moral practice just as much as any other moral claim one might want to make. This latter point, I should note, helps drive home the idea that our moral views are deeply a matter of who we are. We sometimes think that we can step outside our own moral views in order to judge their worth, even their moral worth. But, as I argued earlier, although we may change or develop our moral views, that change always comes from within the context of the current state of a moral practice, not from the outside.

Finally, this section took up the objection that the view I am developing falls prey to a certain kind of relativism. Although there is a form of relativism in this view, it is the nonproblematic relativism of justification, not the more problematic relativism of knowledge.

With this expanded view of the relation between justification and practice now in hand, let's turn to the third example of knowledge that I want to discuss.

YOUR BOSS ONLY HIRED YOU FOR YOUR LOOKS

As this part of the book has unfolded, we have looked more deeply at the issue of knowledge and its inseparability from our practices. We have gone off on a number of side trails, developing the implications of this inseparability, but have always returned to the core idea. As we have done so, we have noticed that in two prominent cases of knowledge—science and morality—the central part of knowledge, justification, is a matter of practices. In this final example, I want to turn to a more pedestrian claim of knowledge, the claim that your boss only hired you for your looks. In this example, too, we will pay attention to how justification is a matter of practices. And as I promised earlier, we'll see a couple of other things as well. First, we'll see how knowing-that is also largely a matter of knowing-how. Second, we'll turn back to the idea of belief, seeing how belief may productively be understood in terms of the related idea of commitment. Finally, we'll see how knowing-how and belief are also closely related.

But before all that, let's take a look at you and your boss. Suppose that I behold you in the office one day, appearing, as usual, arrogant and self-satisfied. You're a man, I'm a woman, and your boss is also a woman. Today I find myself particularly tired of your breezy self-importance. So I happen to mention, while we're standing around the water cooler, that your boss only hired you for your looks. You're stunned. You're not entirely disappointed—since you do pride yourself on your looks—but you're stunned to hear that anyone thinks that your talent ends there. You want to walk away haughtily, but you don't. Instead, you look down at me (being, as you are, not only dark and handsome but also tall) and say, "How would *you* know something like *that*?"

Whatever I say to you at this point, assuming that it involves answering the question and not just upping the ante, will be a justification for my belief that your boss only hired you for your looks. For the sake of the example, let's have at it.

"Look," I say. "She's always leering at you when you walk by, and she stares at your butt when you lean over the copier. She checks through your reports—which she doesn't do for anyone else—and corrects all your lousy mistakes. You didn't have any qualifications for the job in the first place, since this is a job in marketing and your background is in veterinary medicine. And what's more, I heard her comment to another supervisor one day when you walked by that you had the best seat in the house, and that people don't get to import a seat like that all the time."

Well.

These justifications, if true, should certainly help make the case, if not a congenial atmosphere at the water cooler. In order to see what this example is about, let's look at them a little more closely.

One helpful way in which to approach the example is to recognize that it involves two different kinds of practices: the practice of marketing and the practice (or at least one of the practices) of sex. I, your critic, claim to have a more-than-passing knowledge of both. That does not necessarily mean that I am good at marketing, or at sex, but rather that I know what good marketing involves and that I know how the game of sex—at least in the early innings—is played. And, from both my knowledge of these practices and my own observations of the situation, I have concluded that your boss is using the practice of marketing as a cover for really engaging in the practice of sex. (Bear in mind here that the practice of sex does not require that any sexual acts be performed. Sex is a wider, more diffuse practice than that.)

At this point, I hope that you (you as the reader, not you as the boss's sex object) are comfortable with—even if you don't buy—the idea that the structure of knowledge largely involves justification, which occurs in the context of practices. So far, the current example has gone no further than the previous two examples went in developing this idea. The only addition I have tried to make is to import into everyday talk the same treatment of justification that I used in the more cerebral discussions of science and moral theorizing. I don't think that this importation is particularly controversial. Once we get used to the idea that justification is reason-giving in the context of practices, we can apply it just as easily to more pedestrian claims of knowledge as to more theoretical ones.

Taking this example in a slightly different direction, I want us to notice, first, that the inferential moves from the various reasons I gave for my belief to the belief itself—that your boss only hired you for your looks—were pretty quick. Not too quick, just pretty quick. And this distinction between too quick and pretty quick is revealing. When I gave my reasons for believing that your boss only hired you for your looks, you understood them, and understood right away how they could stand as reasons for that belief. That's because you, too, share enough knowledge about the practices of marketing (the example requires fairly little there) and sex (where it requires a bit more) in order to see the inferential connections. Another way to put this point is to say that you know how to move inferentially within these practices at least well enough to follow the reasoning. If I went more deeply into the marketing end of things, I would probably lose many of you (as well as myself) pretty quickly. Regarding the sex, I think I can count on you to stay with me a bit longer, at least epistemically.

This knowing how to move among inferential connections shows us, if we look at it for a moment, how much knowing-that is a matter of knowing-how. Let me put the point in a summary way before developing it: inasmuch as (1) knowing-that involves justification, and (2) justification is a matter of practices, and (3) practices have inferential networks that one must know how to navigate in order to offer justification, then (4) knowing-that is largely (although not exclusively—we haven't discussed truth yet) a matter of knowing-how.

To see this point, recall that knowing-how involves a skill or skills that aren't readily put in the form of claims. One knows how to ride a bike or to navigate a social situation smoothly or to perform a good jazz saxophone solo. The idea I want to press here is that there is another form of knowing-how that is crucial to knowing-that: knowing how to move inferentially through a practice. You know that the boss's staring at your butt at the copier is evidence for the idea that the boss only hired you for your looks, because you know enough about how marketing works and enough about how sex works that you can make that kind of inference. And so it is with inferences in all practices. Being familiar with what kinds of claims link up inferentially with what other kinds of claims in the context of a practice allows you to know what is going on when someone makes a particular claim in that practice. To return to the clitoridectomy example: because you know that something's being oppressive is a reason for its being morally wrong, if I claim that clitoridectomy is oppressive you can immediately conclude that I believe that it is morally wrong (or at least that I believe that there is some strong weight on the side of moral wrongness).

Being raised in a particular society and in the context of its various practices, as we learn the practices we also learn the patterns of reasoning used within them—that is to say, the inferential patterns that those practices employ. We may learn them well, if we are immersed in those practices. Or we may learn them more cursorily, if we are only passingly involved in them. For most of us, for example, the inferential patterns of child rearing become well-learned, while the inferential patterns of marketing or astronomy only more cursorily learned. Some people, of course, become very well-versed in the inferential patterns of particular practices. Those are the people to whom I referred in the first part of this book as the experts in those practices. They know more about the practices because they are more adept at moving inferentially through them. They have a form of know-how that most of the rest of us lack.

So, inasmuch as knowledge (knowledge in its knowing-that form) is a matter of justification, and inasmuch as justification is a matter of making inferences, knowledge—knowing-that—is also a matter of knowing-how. The more know-how you've got regarding the inferential pattern of a particular practice, the more knowledge you're likely to have access to as well. (I say "likely" here to keep before us the idea that knowledge is not simply justification, but involves it.)

Looking at things in this way also helps us understand belief a bit better. Earlier, when addressing belief, I said that at the end of the discussion of justification that I would say something more about belief. This something more would have to do not with what people actually *do* believe, but with what they *ought* to believe, given what else they actually believe. In other words, I wanted to say something more about what people are committed to, given what they believe.

It's now time to take up that task. And the central aspect of that task involves inferential patterns in a practice.

I've been arguing here that there are forms of know-how that are matters of knowing how to move inferentially through various practices. Those kinds of know-how involve knowing what kinds of claims in a practice can serve as reasons for what other kinds of claims. But that's not all that inferential know-how entails. It also involves being able to think about reasons in a practice in a more fine-grained way. More precisely, it involves things like knowing what kinds of claims *permit* but don't require commitment to other kinds of claims, and what kinds of claims *require* commitment to other kinds of claims. Inference, in other words, involves not only reasons but also permissions and requirements.

In order to see how, let me give a couple of examples. Suppose, at the beginning of the baseball season, I know that the Yankees had the best record in the league last year, that most of their players are returning and in good health, that there seems to be no nasty infighting going on, and that George Steinbrenner has decided to take a long vacation from overseeing the team. Under those conditions, you, if you know anything about baseball, would probably agree that I am *permitted* to believe that the Yankees will probably do well this year. I am not *required* to believe it, because I also know that it is hard to repeat a good season and I don't know much about the other teams in the league. But at least I am permitted to infer from the things I do know to the claim that the Yankees will probably do well this year. What we have here is a situation in which I have inferred from certain claims to the conclusion that the Yankees will probably do well this year. This inference is one that is permitted, given the justification, but not required.

If we look back at the example of your boss, we can see that the conclusion of the example—that your boss only hired you for your looks—is also an inference that is permitted, but not required, by the claims that support it. Your boss's treatment of you allows me (but does not require me) to infer that the reason she hired you has to do with something other than the impact your veterinary skills will have on corporate functioning.

Let me turn now to an example of an inference that would be

required in a practice. For the sake of continuity with the example of permitted inferences, let's stick with the practice of baseball. Suppose we're watching a game on television, and I go to the kitchen to get another beer. When I left off watching, the batter had two strikes. As I'm reaching into the fridge, I call out to you, "What happened?" You reply, "He got a third strike." Now, given the rules of baseball, your having claimed that the batter has three strikes against him commits you to claiming that he's out. Not only are you *permitted* to infer that the batter is out from the fact that he has three strikes against him. You are *required* to infer that by the rules of the game. Believing that a hitter has three strikes against him requires that you believe that he is out. There is no other choice.

This is not to say that you actually believe that the batter is out. You *probably* do. After all, why would someone bother watching a baseball game who can't figure out that when you have three strikes you're out? But we can imagine a situation in which you didn't believe that the batter was out. Suppose that you have no interest in baseball and no knowledge of the game. You were only watching the game because you enjoy my company, and I told you that I was going to watch the game today. Suppose further that, in order to bone up on things, you called a friend to find out some basics about baseball. Your friend, just to pull your leg, told you that in baseball you get four strikes and then you're out. Well, in that case you would, in fact, *not* infer from the batter's having three strikes to the batter's being out. Or, to put the issue in terms of belief, you would not believe the batter to be out on the basis of believing that he had three strikes on him. But the *fact* that you didn't believe that the batter was out would not change the normative matter that you were *committed* to believing the batter to be out. In the practice of baseball, having three strikes requires a batter to be out (except in certain unusual circumstances). And in general, certain beliefs or claims performed within the context of a given practice commit one to certain other beliefs or claims tied up with that practice. So, while the practice might not dictate what you actually do or do not believe, it does play a role in deciding what you ought or ought not to believe.

(Of course, the requirements on what one ought or ought not to believe, based on other things one does or does not believe, may change over time. Moreover, it is possible for people in a practice to be mistaken about what one must believe, given what else one believes. But I think I can say with confidence that for any practice we can think of, believing certain things commits one to believing others.)

So where has this discussion taken us? Starting from the example of your boss only hiring you for your looks, we have seen how knowing-that is also a matter of knowing-how, and have looked a bit more at the relation between belief and commitment. Everything that I have said about justification and practices, and much of what we have noted about commitment—if not about belief—relies on the concept of practices. At this point I hope to have been convincing in my case that much of knowledge (and certainly its most interesting aspects) has to do with practices.

We have not, however, discussed truth. In the following section— the last one in this part of the book—I would like to turn to the concept of truth. The perspective on truth that I want to develop, albeit briefly, is a fairly technical one. Its motivating thought is that there isn't anything terribly interesting, at least philosophically, in the concept of truth. If you want to avoid the semi-technical discussion, skipping this section and moving directly to the next part of the book, I can't see any problem with that. But if you do, I'll ask you to take on faith that there is a way in which to conceive the concept of truth that loosens the hold it has had on both philosophers and nonphilosophers over the generations. If you're willing to accept that, and therefore willing to accept that the core issue in knowledge is justification and that justification is a matter of practices, I give you my blessing in turning directly to the third part of the book. For the more skeptical types, here goes.

TRUTH

Let me start by recapping the story thus far. In this part of the book, I've been arguing that knowledge is largely a matter of practices. I've been doing so in order to show how deeply who we are is a matter of our practices. If what we know—or at least what we think we know—is a matter of our practices, then a large part of who we are is also a matter of our practices. There's more, of course. In the first chapter, I talked about the role of practices in what I do and in how I think about and relate to myself and to others. In the third chapter, I'll relate practices to morality and to politics. But here I'm concerned with knowledge.

So far, I've tried to show how the kinds of beliefs we have and the reasons for them are importantly tied to our practices. What I have not done is argue that the *truth* of our beliefs is tied to our practices. And for good reason: if I argued that the truth of our beliefs was tied to our practices, I'd be wrong. Not only would I be wrong, but I'd also be incoherent.

Why?

For the reason I gave earlier, when I said that while relativism about justification is perfectly coherent, relativism about knowledge is not. Let's suppose that I tell you, "All truth is relative to practices." It's perfectly reasonable for you to ask me whether that claim itself is relative to a particular practice or other. If it isn't, then it's false to say that all truth is relative to practices, because the (purportedly true) claim "All truth is relative to practices" is *not* relative to a practice. On the other hand, if the claim is said to be true relative to certain practices, then that would leave open the possibility that it is false relative to other practices. So it would be false to say that *all* truth is relative to certain practices. Either way—regardless of whether the claim is said to be relative to certain practices—the claim doesn't work out. It's a claim that possesses a certain self-contradictory character, like the claim "I always lie."

But that isn't the only problem with a view that holds truth to be relative to practices. Disregarding the logical problem, there are some good practical reasons for avoiding that view as well. For instance, it was once believed that the earth was flat. That belief was justified relative to the scientific practices at that time. Let's say we want to hold that truth is relative to the practices of a certain time. Would we want to say that the belief "The earth is flat" was true at that time? Certainly, it *seemed* true relative to the practices of the time. But the earth wasn't any flatter back then than it is now. So it would be wrong to say that the truth of the claim "The earth is flat" is relative to any practice.

In response to this, someone might want to say, "Well, the claim 'The earth is flat' was true in a sense. It was true *for them*. And it's not true for us. So truth *is* relative to certain practices. The claim 'The earth is flat' is true relative to the scientific practices of some hundreds of years ago, and not true relative to the scientific practices of today."

This is a tempting response, but I don't think that it will work. Here's why. The idea of "true for them" seems to be the same as "they believed it," or at most, "they believed it with justification." In other words, if we respond with the "true for them" option, we seem to reduce knowledge to justified belief. Truth just drops out of the equation. And I don't think that we want truth to drop out of the equation. We want to have a way of saying things like, "They believed it, and with good reason, but it wasn't true."

Why do we want to have a way of saying things like that? We have already seen that when I judge a claim, I do so from the perspective of the practices I endorse or in which I am engaged. That's one of the things it means to endorse or to be engaged in a practice: to take the inferential patterns of the practice seriously. (As we have also seen, it doesn't mean that one blindly ratifies all aspects of the inferential pattern; it means that one does not question all of it at the same time. There is a certain wholeness to the pattern that one endorses.) So when I evaluate the truth or falsity of a claim, I do so relative to justifications that lie within certain practices. But, from the perspective of those practices—or at least of my way of taking them up—certain claims look to me to be true and others look to be false. They *don't* look to me to be true or false relative to my practice. They look to me to be true or false, period.

Why? Because I endorse the practice that forms the basis of judgment for the claim in question. To refer to our example, when I say that it is false that the earth is flat, or true that the earth is round, I'm not saying, "It's false that the earth is flat (or true that the earth is round) relative to the scientific practices I endorse." It is, of course, right to say that, relative to the scientific practices I endorse, it is false that the earth is flat and true that the earth is round. But *that's not what I'm saying.* I'm not saying, "Given the scientific practices I endorse, the earth is round, not flat." I'm saying, "The earth is round, not flat."

To put the point succinctly: while it may be right to say that the reasons one holds a belief to be true or false are relative to the practices one endorses or engages in (that's been my argument for most of this part of the book), when one says that a claim is true or false, one is not making any claims about one's practices. One is making claims about the way things are. Or, to get at the issue another way, although our beliefs about truth and falsity are based upon the justifications we give ourselves, our claims of truth and falsity are not claims *about* those justifications. They are claims about the world, or about us, or about something else—but not about our justifications.

On this line of thinking, then, we need the idea of truth in order to be able to say things that it would be difficult to say otherwise. If we develop this concept, then we will understand truth not as some philosophically deep matter, but as something that allows us to make certain linguistic moves that we wouldn't otherwise make. These would include moves like, "Back in the Middle Ages, people were justified in thinking that the earth was flat, but it still isn't true that it was," or "What John said about computers improving our lives is true, but his reasons for it are all screwed up."

I want to develop this approach to truth a bit, but before doing so, I will engage in a couple of preliminaries. First, the view of truth I want to endorse here comes from two sources, both listed in the bibliography: Robert Brandom's *Making It Explicit* and, particularly, Grover, Camp, and Belnap's article, "A Prosentential Theory of Truth." (For readers who want to see this view laid out in proper technical detail, those are the places to look.)

Second, in order to get hold of what is going on in this view of truth, it wouldn't hurt to contrast it with another view. Perhaps the best candidate for contrast is the most commonly held view of truth, the correspondence theory. There are many other theories of truth—for example, the coherence and pragmatist theories—but the correspondence theory is by far the most widely held view of truth, and likely the best one to compare with the view of truth that I want to present.

The correspondence theory of truth, at least in its basic formulation, is simple. It says that truth consists of the correspondence of
claims to states of affairs. Otherwise put, what makes a claim true is
that it corresponds to the way things are. Truth, then, is a matter of
the link between what one says (or writes) and what happens to be
the case "out there," or "in the world," or "in reality."

On the face of it, the correspondence theory of truth seems
straightforwardly plausible. If I make some sort of claim, wouldn't it
be the case that that claim is true if it somehow reflects or hooks up
with the ways things really are in the world? For instance, if I say,
"The Mazda Miata I saw last week cost $25,000," what would make
that claim true would be that it hooks up with the Mazda Miata in the
right way—in this case, if it hooks up in the way of the Miata's
costing $25,000. If, in fact, the Miata does (or at least did) cost
$25,000, then the state of affairs does correspond to what I said, and
my claim is true. If not, then my claim is false. To summarize the
point, the Miata's costing $25,000 would *make* the claim true; its not
costing $25,000 would *make* the claim false.

Now, there is something right in what the correspondence theory
wants to put forward, and then again there is something problematic
as well. It is surely right to say that if the Miata actually cost $25,000,
then my claim is true; otherwise, it is false. That captures something
about the idea of truth, and is perhaps the reason that the correspondence theory is so popular. But what is problematic is the idea of the
correspondence, the idea that I have variously labeled "link," "hook,"
"reflect," and "make." How does this correspondence occur? In what
way, we might ask, does the way things are actually *make* a claim true?
What is the nature of the *link* between words and the world that gives
truthfulness to those words? What form does this *reflection* of a statement into a state of affairs take? How do claims *hook* onto things (or
vice versa) such that we wind up with truth?

We can readily admit that the claim "The Mazda Miata I saw last
week cost $25,000" is true if and only if the Mazda Miata I saw last
week cost $25,000. No problem there. But the correspondence theory
of truth says something more on behalf of truth. And it's the more
part that creates all the difficulties. It says that the Miata's costing

$25,000 somehow makes the words true, that the fact somehow hooks onto the words in a way that yields truthfulness, and that truth is a particular kind of quality (correspondence) that emerges in this making or this hooking. That's the problematic part.

So what's the problem? It isn't incoherent to say that there is this correspondence. We certainly don't have, for instance, the kind of incoherence that attaches to the relativist view of truth we just saw. Rather, the problem is one of mystery. No philosopher has succeeded in telling a plausible story about what the correspondence is supposed to be. No one has offered a reasonable view of what constitutes the correspondence. While the idea of a correspondence seems to be sort of catchy, the ability to identify what this idea is all about has turned out to be pretty elusive.

This is not to say that one *couldn't* perhaps come up with a story about correspondence that will work. I don't want to claim that there can't be a philosophical account of correspondence. But nobody has yet come up with one in many hundreds of years of trying, and the prospects don't look good. So while the idea that the claim "*x* is the case" is true if and only if *x* is the case is easy to accept, the idea of *x*'s being the case *making* the claim true is a little more difficult. And even if one could tell a story that would work in a particular instance, why should we believe that that story would serve as a general story about truth? Why, for instance, should we believe that snow's being white makes the claim "Snow is white" true *in the same way* that the Miata's costing $25,000 makes my claim "The Mazda Miata I saw last week cost $25,000" true?

I think that one of the reasons the correspondence theory of truth has continued to hold sway over people's imaginations is that we think of truth as a Big Philosophical Item. We think that the idea of truth holds mysteries for us that, if we can solve them, will tell us something profound about the nature of the world in which we live, and specifically about the relations between our minds or our language and the world. We tend to think of truth as Truth, as a vast area on the philosophical landscape, a puzzle that must be solved in order for us to get hold of who we are and where we (and the world) are. As long as we continue to think in this way, the idea of a correspondence that occurs between our words and the world will appear to us as an important philosophical problem that requires a deep philosophical solution. As with many philosophical issues, we are in the grip of an idea that seems to have real weight, even though we can't exactly locate that weight.

My suggestion is that we give up this idea. Instead of thinking of truth as a Big Philosophical Item, let's think of it as a useful linguistic one. I have already tried to convince you that the philosophically interesting part of knowledge has to do with justification. Now I'll try to give you a thumbnail account of truth that goes along with that idea. It's called a "deflationary" account, because it deflates the importance of truth as a philosophical problem. (Philosophy as balloon science.) There are several important deflationary accounts of truth floating around the philosophical community these days. Frankly, all of them (or at least all of the ones I know about) would work well with the perspective on knowledge I'm developing here. The following one, the prosentential theory, is the one on which I was brought up, and the one for which I have the most sympathy.

The prosentential theory of truth can be seen as one of the offspring of the redundancy theory of truth. The redundancy theory of truth holds the idea of truth to be simply a redundancy. For instance, there is no difference in content between my saying "Nouvelle cuisine is no longer new" and my saying "It's true that nouvelle cuisine is no longer new." They both say the same thing. Adding the "It's true that . . ." to the beginning of the second sentence is redundant.

You can see right away why this is a deflationary approach to truth. Far from saying that there is some deep mystery to truth, it denies that the idea of truth performs any function whatsoever, except perhaps to second the motion of some claim that has already been made.

However, there is a problem with the redundancy theory of truth. If truth is redundant, then presumably it can be eliminated from a sentence without the sentence changing what it is saying. So, in the above example, if I remove the "It's true that . . ." part from the second sentence, I'm left with "Nouvelle cuisine is no longer new," which says the same thing that the sentence "It's true that nouvelle cuisine is no longer new" does. So far, so good. But the idea that we can subtract the "truth" part of a sentence without changing the sentence at all doesn't work for all sentences.

Consider, for instance, the sentence, "Everything Todd says about practices is true." Now, subtract the truth part. All you have left is "Everything Todd says about practices." That isn't even a sentence, much less the same sentence as the original one. So truth can't be completely redundant. There must be something more to it. But can we give an account of that something more without having to go back to the idea that truth is somehow philosophically deep?

As it turns out, we can.

The prosentential theory of truth tries to preserve the general take on truth that characterized the redundancy theory, but without that theory's philosophical problems. The prosentential theory states that locutions like "It's true" and "That's true" serve as *prosentences,* in much the same way that "he" or "it" serve as pronouns. Here's how it works. A pronoun is a stand-in for a proper name that isn't being said. For example, suppose I ask you, "Where's John?" and you reply, "He's at the store." The "he" in your sentence in a stand-in for the name "John." It refers to the "John" in my sentence. We can call it an "intralinguistic reference" (or, in the term used by Grover et al. and Brandom, an "anaphor"), because it is referring to another word previously used. In this case, the previously used word is "John."

Prosentences work in much the same way, except that instead of referring to proper names, they refer to whole sentences. So if you say, "The boss only hired that guy for his looks," and I reply, "That's true," it's as though I've just repeated your sentence by referring to the whole thing. Using this idea of intralinguistic reference allows us to give an account of truth that deflates its philosophical importance without leaving us wondering whether the idea of truth has any role to play at all.

Consider, for instance, the kind of sentence that tripped up the redundancy theory: "Everything Todd says about practices is true." What the prosentential theory says is that such a sentence is referring to all sentences I've said about practices. It's repeating them, as it were. And think of how convenient that makes things. Instead of having to make a large list of everything I've said and then affirming it, having locutions like "It's true" and "That's true" and ". . . is true" allows us quickly and efficiently to do a lot of referring to what other people have said.

Imagine what it would be like if we wanted to say that everything I said about practices is true, but we couldn't use any words associated with truth. We'd have to do something like this: "Todd said that practices were socially normatively governed . . . and indeed they are; and Todd said that our knowledge is largely determined by our practices, and indeed it is; and Todd said . . . , and he was right about that." Isn't it a whole lot easier to have a way of grouping all that stuff together and saying it at the same time? That's what the various locutions around truth allow us to do. Instead of having to make individual references to specific sentences, we can refer to them quickly or as an entire group.

It's not as though we couldn't say the same things we already say without all the various locutions around truth, just as we could still say everything we needed to say without our language's possessing any pronouns. But linguistic life is a lot easier with pronouns and prosentences. Rather than having to engage in cumbersome repetition, we get to navigate our linguistic world more smoothly by using such locutions as "That's true" or "Everything he said is true."

It also allows us to do the kinds of things I pointed out at the beginning of this section, to say things like, "Hundreds of years ago, people were justified in saying that the earth was flat, but it wasn't true." In this case, I make a distinction between justification (which is a matter of practices) and truth (which isn't), saying that although it was at one time justified to think that the earth is flat, the earth is not flat. To put the point in another way, I distinguish between what I am willing to believe was justified at one time and what I am willing to ratify myself. Locutions around truth allow this to happen more easily than they would otherwise.

As it turns out, there is a phrase from current slang that captures the prosentential theory of truth exactly: "what he said." You may be familiar with this phrase. Suppose somebody we both know is giving his view of some matter or another, and you want to know what I think of it. When you ask me, I respond, "What he said." What else am I doing but using a short sentence to refer to and ratify *what he said?* The sentence can also be used without being prompted by a question. Suppose, for instance, this person is saying things that I agree with completely and wholeheartedly. At the end of his talk, I might spontaneously say, "What he said!" In doing that, I refer to all the things he said and, in a way, say them again in my own voice. I do this without having to go over everything he said sentence by sentence. On the prosentential theory of truth, truth works just like that. It refers to other sentences, repeating them without having to go to the (sometimes extreme) bother of saying each one another time.

For some, this deflationary view of truth might seem, well, deflating. It might come off like a cheap technical trick used to deal with a long-standing philosophical issue without having to do the real work of confronting the problem. And there's no question that it is a way of trying to deflate any philosophical issues associated with truth. But remember that this approach to truth is embedded into a much larger approach to knowledge that does see many interesting philosophical issues tied up with knowledge. Those issues are tied up with justification rather than with truth. So it's not as though I don't think that there is any philosophy to be done around the issue of knowledge. Rather, I think we need to shift the ground of philosophical inquiry from truth to justification in order to get clear on how knowledge works.

Sometimes, the beginning of philosophical wisdom lies in pinpointing the interesting problems. In this case, what people like Grover et al. and Brandom have done is to allow us to see those interesting problems by pointing away from a false problem. If we can stop relying on truth as the guide to the concept of knowledge, and can look instead at justification, then we can start down a road that, I believe, will lead us to greater philosophical understanding—of our knowledge, our practices, and ourselves—than will the road many of us traveled in the past, seeking our understanding from the nature of truth.

What I have tried to do in this part of the book is to paint a picture of knowledge that moves away from foundations to practices and, in a related gesture, from truth to justification. In doing so, we have seen that what we believe is more deeply bound to what we do than previous accounts had admitted, and we have begun to trace the outlines of a holistic view, one that sees who we are, what we do, and what we have reason to believe all converging (at least largely) on the practices in which we are engaged. In the final part of the book, I want to turn from knowledge to action (while recognizing that these are not separate, but entwined), and to investigate the relation of practices to morality and to politics.

3

OUR PRACTICES, OUR MORALS, AND OUR POLITICS

THINKING ABOUT MORALITY

In this chapter, the discussion will turn from what philosophers often call *epistemic* concerns (concerns about knowledge) to what they call *normative* ones (concerns about rules, norms, and action). From the perspective of practices, the distinction between the epistemic and the normative is not nearly as great as it might seem. In the previous part of the book, we saw examples of both the normative nature of the epistemic and the epistemic nature of the normative. We saw the normative nature of the epistemic when we considered what one *ought* to be committed to believing, given other things one believes. We saw the epistemic nature of the normative in the discussion of morality, at which point I argued that moral theorizing is a matter of knowledge just as scientific theorizing is.

In thinking about morality, however, we should not confuse all morality with moral theorizing. When people act morally, they don't always do so as a result of a reflective process of thinking about the moral rights and wrongs of a situation, deciding what to do, and then doing it. In fact, that kind of moral action is probably the exception rather than the rule. Most of the time, people have a sense of how they ought to act, and they go ahead and act that way without having to put much thought into it. Moral theorizing, then, is not the only source of moral action. It isn't even the usual source.

If, then, the practice of moral theorizing is only one of the sources of moral action, what other sources are there? How does morality work in our lives, and why do we act in accordance with it? In order to answer these questions, we'll need to think broadly about values in their relation to practices. From the general idea of values, we can turn back to specifically moral values and then see how they work.

As always, however, let me start with some preliminaries, in this case a couple of words about values. First, the sense in which I want to use the term *value* is in application to people's doings and ways of being and the kinds of situations those doings and ways of being promote. We can, of course, think of objects as having value. We say, for instance, that a Ming-dynasty vase has great value. In that case, by "value" we mean aesthetic or monetary value. But those aren't synonymous with the type of value in which I'm interested here. If we are going to work our way toward morality, we want to think of values as being tied up with how people act and who they are rather than with objects. For our purposes then, the term *value* will not refer to objects but to acts and ways of being and their consequences.

The second word about values is this. There is, of course, a distinction that can be made between being a value and having value. For example, it is often said that the good or the right *is* a value, while promoting the good or the right *has* value. For our purposes, however, the distinction is not that important, so I'm going to run roughshod over it. In most cases, when I talk about values, I'll be referring to something's having value, rather than being a value. But the use of the words "having value" can become grammatically awkward at spots, in which case I'll just call something a value for the sake of ease. If it looks as though I'm playing a little fast and loose with the distinction here, it's because I am. I don't think anything we need to see hangs on this distinction, so I believe I can get away with it.

With these preliminaries out of the way, we can now begin to grapple with the issues.

Different practices embody or at least endorse different values. For instance, hunting embodies values of manhood, outdoorsmanship, and, when it is done properly, respect for nature. Psychotherapy embodies personal reflectiveness and self-knowledge. Churchgoing often (but not always) endorses values of humility, obedience to a transcendent authority, and community. So some of the values of a practice are tied up with its goals. Clearly, the goals a practice has in view are considered worthy of promoting and thus have value. But along the way, a practice may develop values that are related to its goals but are not reducible to them. In the case of hunting, the value of respecting nature is perhaps a helpful value for hunters to have; after all, if nature is disrespected, where will they hunt? However, it is not necessary to the goals of hunting as a sport or as an attempt to obtain food that nature be respected. There are, of course, plenty of hunters who have no respect for nature and are still able to accomplish the goals of the practice. I don't think that those hunters should elicit our respect, but that doesn't mean that they aren't part of the practice of hunting—just as reckless drivers are still engaged in the practice of driving. We may, then, think of a practice as involving values that are often related—but not always reducible—to the values directly linked to the goals of that practice.

Is it possible that there are values that arise or exist outside of the practices in which people engage? Or are values necessarily part of practices? As a matter of logical possibility, I think that it is indeed possible to have values that are outside all practices; as a practical matter, however, values seem to be necessarily bound to practices. Let me offer an example of a value someone might hold that is not related to any particular practice. Let's suppose that I like ice cream. A lot. A *whole* lot. I might, because of this, hold the eating of ice cream to be a value. Not the making of it, which would be an engagement in a practice. No, what I think is valuable is the eating of ice cream, which doesn't necessarily have to be bound to some particular type of practice. In this case, I seem to be embracing a value that is not tied up with practices.

But note—no doubt you already have—how strange the example had to be in order for me to come up with a case of a value unrelated to a practice. Practically speaking, values appear to be inextricably intertwined with the practices in which people engage, for a reason that should become evident as I clear up a potential confusion in the example we just saw.

The potential confusion is this. In the case of the person who thinks of eating ice cream as having value, what that person is thinking is not simply that he (or she) likes eating ice cream. There is a difference between "values" and "likes." *Likes* are personal, in the sense that a like isn't something you necessarily think of as good for anyone other than yourself. *Values* are goods that are more general. When we think of something as a value or as having value, we are thinking that it would be good if other people were engaged in it. In that way, values are social rather than personal.

Seeing this point, we can also see why it is that values tend toward practices. It is in engagement with others that values (as distinguished from likes) arise, because values have to do with others and not just ourselves. And since, as I argued in the first part of the book, much of our social life is a matter of the practices in which we engage, values are then deeply tied to practices. (This idea of values being tied to practices is one that the philosopher James Wallace follows in detail in his book *Ethical Norms, Particular Cases*. Wallace's approach to values and morality is a lot like mine, although they're not identical. For those who would like to pursue this line of thinking about morality further, Wallace's book is an excellent place to start.)

Let me turn now from values generally to specifically moral values. Some of the values we discussed—say, outdoorsmanship in hunting or obedience to a transcendent authority in churchgoing—do not seem to have the status of moral values. Those values are tied closely to the practices in which they appear. Of course, the same value can appear in other practices as well, but these practices are often related to one another in important ways. For instance, outdoorsmanship emerges in the practices of camping and rock climbing as well as that of hunting.

But the obvious affinities among those three practices make the appearance of the same value in all three unsurprising.

There are other values, however, that do not seem to be restricted to particular practices or groups of practices. We would say that values in this latter category are worth embracing regardless of the practices in which one is engaged. Respect for others, telling the truth, and keeping one's promises, for example, are values that one finds in almost every practice one can imagine. These values are, in a sense we have yet to explore, *universal* values. And it is the universal values that are the moral values.

Before turning to the universality of moral values, let me pause to dispel another potential confusion before it arises: the confusion of universal values with absolute ones. Given the examples of moral values I've chosen—respecting others, telling the truth, keeping one's promises—you might want to raise an objection: "Wait a minute, those values can't hold true all the time. There are cases in which keeping one's promise would not be the morally right thing to do. Suppose, for instance, I've promised to meet you for coffee, and on the way I see some innocent person getting attacked and I stop to help that person. I might be breaking my promise to you, but that doesn't mean that I've done the morally wrong thing. In fact, I did the morally right thing by helping to stop the attack."

True enough. To call a value a universal value (or, to lapse into precision about values for a moment, to say of an act that it embodies or promotes a universal value) is not the same thing as saying that it is (or embodies, or promotes) an absolute value. An absolute value is a value that cannot be overridden. A universal value, in contrast, is a value that is applicable or relevant everywhere. A value can certainly be universal without being absolute. It can be universal in the sense that it is applicable or relevant to every situation in which it arises, even though it can be overridden by more important considerations (which themselves often turn out to be universal ones).

(As to the question of whether a value can be absolute but not universal, I believe that the answer here is *no*. Absolute values would presumably be absolute because of their importance, and therefore would demand the kind of universal recognition that is associated with moral values. It may well be, of course, that a value some people hold as absolute is not universally accepted. In that case, those people would be committed to thinking that the others who fail to recognize this value are mistaken.)

The charitable action I just ascribed to you is a good case in point. In that scenario, there are actually two values in play: the value of keeping promises and the value of helping to protect the innocent. These are both values that are universal (in a sense still to be fully explained). But in this case, the value of helping to protect the innocent overrides the value of keeping one's promise. It's not that keeping one's promise is irrelevant to the situation. It *is* relevant, just not overriding. Or, to put the point in a different way, the promise has moral weight, but not as much moral weight as helping the innocent. It matters—matters morally—that you made a promise to me. And, had things been different, you ought to have kept that promise. But it matters more that there is an innocent person being attacked, and therefore your promise to me, while relevant, is not overriding. Keeping one's promises, then, is a universal value, but not an absolute one.

Now here one might want to ask for an example of an absolute value. That seems to me to be a difficult request to which to respond adequately. I can think of candidates for answers, but they all seem to exist at such a level of generality that they offer no real moral guidance. For instance, not torturing babies just for fun strikes me as about as close to an absolute value as one would want to imagine. But, confronted with such a value, one is tempted to say, "So what? Who's thinking of torturing babies just for fun in the first place?" And, I think, that would be the right response. Absolute values are often morally empty, not in the sense that they don't tell us anything at all, but in the sense that they don't give us the kinds of guidance we need from morality. Rather than looking for absolute values, a better approach to morality is usually to look for universal values and then to see how they weigh against one another in a given situation.

Which brings us to a new question: What is a universal value? I want to define a *universal value* as a value that is relevant regardless of the practice (or non-practice) in which one is engaged. A universal value is a value that is applicable across practices, and even in contexts in which one is not engaged in a practice—as rare as those might be.

Let me distinguish this definition from another definition that might be confused with it (and that I want to avoid like the plague). That other definition would see a universal value as a value that exists independently of all practices. A moment's reflection will convince us that, given the perspective I'm developing here, that second definition won't do. First, it seems to have a foundationalist flavor, in a way that offends the antifoundationalism of the previous part of this book. What seems to be sought in a universal value that exists independently of all practices is some sort of transcendent truth, something outside our social relations and engagements that would provide a moral foundation for them. And just as foundationalism about knowledge seems to be a hopeless project, so does foundationalism about universal values.

The other problem with this way of defining universal values is that it abstracts them too far from our practices, and I don't think that values either arise or are applied in that way. Why not? Well, certainly one of the most central purposes of morality—if not *the* central purpose—is to give us guidance in our social relations. But in order to give guidance in social relations, morality is going to have to be responsive to what those social relations are. And if, as I have been arguing, most of our social relations are determined by our practices (and our individual ways of engaging in those practices), then morality is going to have to be responsive to those practices. So it would seem that as moral values arise and change, they do so (at least in good part) in response to the evolution of practices in a particular society and the requirements that such an evolution imposes on that society. Moreover, the character of morality's responsiveness to practices will yield universal values that are applicable across a society's practices at a given time. Those values won't be absolute, and they won't be unchanging, but they will be universal. In short, the values will offer general social guidance across practices in a particular social arrangement.

In order to see how this can be, let me take two values and look at their role in our practices. The first—the value of truth telling—has remained relatively unchanged over time. The second—the value of respecting one's class status and the class status of others—has, at least in a formal (if not actual) sense, all but disappeared in many parts of the world. I want to use the first one to illustrate how moral values, as opposed to other values, are applicable not only within practices but also across them. The second will illustrate the changing nature of moral values.

I hope that I can count on all of us to recognize truth telling as a moral value. Now think of how truth telling differs from, say, outdoorsmanship. We think of outdoorsmanship as a value for certain people, but not necessarily binding on everyone. I, for instance, as a child of New York, have no place for outdoorsmanship in my behavioral repertoire. I have no difficulty in respecting it in others and in recognizing how it might have value for them. In some cases, I even admire it. But for me, forget about it. With truth telling, however, things are different. I expect myself to tell the truth, and I expect others to do so. Truth telling is a value that I—and, I suppose, others—believe to be applicable to those who are and those who aren't outdoor types. Otherwise put, while outdoorsmanship is not a universal value, truth telling is. And my suggestion here is that when we think about morality, or think in terms of morality, we are thinking about or in terms of values that we believe to be applicable across practices, not merely within some of them.

Universality, however, does not require timelessness any more than it requires absoluteness. At one time, respecting one's place in a class society was considered an important and universal value. Members of a particular class were expected to talk to and act toward other members of their own class in certain ways, ways that were very distinct from the ways in which they were expected to talk to and act toward members of other classes. Those ways of speaking and acting were quite rigid, and it was considered immoral to use the same types of speech or behavior across classes. For a peasant to talk to an aristocrat in the same way in which he or she talked to another peasant would have been considered an act of trying to rise above one's station, which was morally blameworthy. Conversely, for an aristocrat to talk to a peasant just as he or she would talk to another aristocrat would have been thought of as a failure or refusal to recognize the fundamental differences among people, differences that were often talked about in terms of bloodlines. That failure or refusal would have been considered a moral one.

I don't want to argue here that we no longer have classes in the world, or even in the United States. In fact, although I won't linger over this point, it seems to me that we clearly do have classes. What we no longer have is a set of formal requirements to regulate how in-class and out-class talk and behavior should go. And we no longer have the kinds of beliefs about rising above one's station and fundamental blood differences among people that undergirded earlier requirements placed upon class behavior. Of course, we still have something like different ways of speaking and acting, as anyone who is poor and has attended an upper-class social function will immediately recognize. But these differences are no longer the subject of moral sanction as they were in recent centuries. At most, they are matters of etiquette. A person who cannot engage in the class talk and behavior is guilty, not of a moral lapse, but of an ignorance about "how we do things around here."

I hope that these two examples offer some idea of what moral values are and how they differ from other kinds of values. Based on this discussion, however, one might be tempted to revisit an objection that I tried to deal with in the last part of the book, in the section on the relativist nature of morality. If moral values are neither absolute nor unchanging, one might ask, then to what extent would anyone be justified in saying that they are universal? Previously, I argued that moral claims ought to be taken as matters of knowledge in much the same way that scientific claims are. I also argued that the facts of moral disagreement and of cultural differences in morality do not necessarily lead to any type of moral relativism. In fact, I claimed that an embrace of a relativism regarding the truth of moral claims was self-defeating.

However, the worry that drove the objections in the last part of the book could reappear here in a different guise. Here's how it would go: "Okay, relativism about morality is self-defeating. But if we are going to hold moral claims to be true, and at the same time hold moral values to be universal, then which values get to be the universal ones? Moreover, if justification happens only within the context of practices, and if moral values are supposed to be applied across practices, how are we going to get a set of universal values that works even within the context of one culture, never mind across cultures?" To put the question in another way: if justification is, as it were, practice-specific, how will the universality of moral values have a claim across various practices?

The short answer to this question is that there is a single practice—the practice of moral theorizing referred to in the last part of the book—that is the seat of such universalizing. But that short answer will lead us down some important pathways, important enough that they need a separate section.

MORAL THEORIZING AND MORAL CONFLICT

In the previous part of the book, I said that moral theorizing was a distinct practice. Not all morality, of course, involves moral theorizing. In fact, we engage in most of our moral behavior without any theorizing at all. Moral theorizing appears on the scene only when there is some uncertainty about how we ought to act, when we need to reflect more deeply on a situation in order to know what to do. As I tell my students in business ethics, you don't need a moral theory to tell you not to knock old people down when they're crossing the street. You need a moral theory—or at least some moral thought—when you don't know how you ought to act. Moral theorizing arises when you have a moral dilemma.

In the last section I said that moral values are those values that apply not only within practices but across them as well. The question was then raised of how to tell which values are applicable across practices. This question is especially urgent, since I have been denying all along that justification can occur outside practices. Therefore, the question of which values are applicable across practices must itself be raised within the context of a particular practice. And indeed it is. It is raised within the practice of moral theorizing.

Now we needn't think of moral theorizing as necessarily involving the appeal to deep abstract theories about human motivation, the problem of evil, the nature of the right and the good, or the structure of moral responsibility. For philosophers, of course, such issues matter. And one hopes that the kinds of reflections that philosophers engage in about these matters will help develop everyday moral theorizing in fruitful ways. (However, as I noted at the outset, given the state of philosophical discussion and the marginalization of philosophy generally, this hope is unlikely to be fulfilled anytime soon.) But moral theorizing can be done by anyone who is capable of reflecting on the rights and wrongs of human behavior.

Let me offer an example here to illustrate the pedestrian kinds of things that can count as engagements in the practice of moral theorizing. Suppose you get called one evening by a married friend of yours who invites you out for a drink. At the bar, your friend reveals to you that he has been having an affair that his wife doesn't know about. He asks you not to tell his wife about it, because it would be too upsetting to her and because the affair is not a serious one and because it is ending anyway since the woman is leaving town. Now you are also friends with the wife, perhaps good friends. What do you do?

As you can see, there is no obviously correct course of action here. On the one hand, there is the issue of loyalty to the wife, which might come down in favor of telling her. Anger against your friend for putting you in this dilemma is probably in play, too, although that isn't a good reason for telling. On the other hand, what might revealing the affair to her do to the marriage, especially since you aren't privy to all the details about how this marriage is going anyway? It's clear that you have to make some sort of a decision. You can't pretend that you didn't know about the affair—at least not to yourself. So you weigh the positives and negatives of telling and you make a decision one way or the other.

In thinking about what you ought to do, and then coming to a decision (or further indecision), you were engaged in the practice of moral theorizing. You didn't necessarily come up with an overarching moral theory—a theory about what kinds of things are morally right and wrong in general. In fact, you most likely didn't, although you may have been engaged in thinking in ways that converge with one moral theory or another. For instance, you may have wondered what would cause the most good, as utilitarians do, or you may have wondered whether you would want to have been told if you were the wife, as Kantian deontologists do. But you probably didn't ask yourself consciously theoretical questions. Most likely, you just weighed the kinds of moral pros and cons that bore on the situation, asked yourself about your duties to the various parties involved and the effects of telling and of not telling, and then made a decision to go ahead or to shut up.

But in doing that, you engaged in the practice that I am calling "moral theorizing." You moved from a more or less unconscious automatic moral action to a more reflective weighing and deliberating. And in doing that, you no longer took for granted—because, given the situation, you couldn't—an unreflective reliance on such moral advice as "Don't betray your friends" or "Respect the privacy of others." In this case, those moral rules of thumb don't apply straight-forwardly. So instead of acting right away, you had to think out the morally right thing to do. You had to decide which moral rules of thumb were more important than which others, or which conse-quences of what you might do or not do were better than others, and why. And in doing that, you were participating in the practice of moral theorizing.

Philosophers who do moral theorizing are engaged in the same practice. Usually, although not always, they are engaged in it at a more abstract level; it is still the same practice, however. In applied ethics, the level is usually less abstract. In the creation of overall moral theories, it is more abstract. But it is still recognizably the same prac-tice. For instance, a philosopher might come up with a general theory of the good that, among other things, offers an explanation of why it is that respecting privacy is more important than being privy to a betrayal. Such a theory would offer an analysis of the good at a high level of abstraction, but that analysis would probably issue out into more specific moral advice. In this way, we might consider moral philosophers the experts in moral theorizing, in much the same way that we consider biologists the experts in biology. That doesn't mean that moral philosophers are actually any better than anyone else is, morally speaking (any more than biologists actually live better than anyone else does). It's just that they know more about how to reflect morally than most of the rest of us do.

The upshot of this discussion so far is that moral theorizing is a recognizable practice whose purpose is to navigate moral dilemmas. I haven't said just how it is that moral theorizing works with universal values, as opposed to the values of just its own practice, but standing where we are now, that's fairly easy to see. One begins moral theorizing when the move to make in one's own practice (such as the practice of teaching) is unclear to one. That's just what it is to feel oneself to be in a moral dilemma. And so, what does one do? One removes oneself from the immediate engagement in the practice and into the more reflective practice of moral theorizing. One comes up with an answer, and then returns to the practice. That's just what you did in the example we were turning over a moment ago. (Of course, one doesn't need to be involved in a practice in order to be in a moral dilemma—but, if the general direction of this book is right, being involved in a practice will be the usual starting point.)

Now, if the practice of moral theorizing is the practice you turn to in cases of moral dilemmas, regardless of the practice in which you're participating when the dilemma arises, then that must be because the values involved in moral theorizing are applicable to any practice in which you participate. Or, to put it another way, that must be because moral values are universal. The practice of moral theorizing intersects with any number of other practices, because the values it works with—and thus the values that anyone works with in trying to solve moral dilemmas—are applicable to all practices (and even to those unusual situations in which no practice is involved). Some practices intersect with others because they have values in common. But moral theorizing intersects with all practices because its values are applicable to all practices.

One can see the advantage, for general social stability and coordination, of having values that apply to all practices. After all, people often participate in very divergent practices. And the more divergent the practices, the less people have in common. (This is particularly true in a technologically advanced society, but it probably holds to one degree or another for almost all societies.) How, then, do people who are coming from divergent practices, with their divergent beliefs and inferential structures and patterns of behavior, interact? How do they navigate the social space between them? Well, if there are some universal principles in the society, then there are certain basic rules to start from and certain norms one can count on in order to coordinate social relations. This helps keep things from getting chaotic.

Social coordination is not the only point of having universal values, however. If so, then morality would be relativist in the way that I rejected in the last part of the book, because its values would hold good only for the society they are helping to coordinate. Universal values also respond to deep intuitions we have about how life should go, about what creatures are deserving of respect, about what human beings owe one another as a matter of course, and the like. The practice of moral theorizing, then, is not only a practical one, in the sense of helping us navigate our society more smoothly. It is also a matter of who we consider ourselves to be, and what orientation toward the world and toward others we see ourselves and others as needing to take. In contrast to values that are more practice-specific, moral values reflect what people think others deserve regardless of their interests and their engagements. Believing that people ought to have their autonomy respected, or that they ought to tell the truth, involves concerns about *how* any human life ought to go, concerns that do not end at the borders of one's own society or culture. That is why moral values apply not only across the practices of a given society but also in a more universal way, across the practices of *all* societies.

Let me be clear here. I am not arguing that there is a particular set of moral values that everyone in the world can agree on that will hold across societies. Far from it. My suggestion is that for a value to be considered a moral value by someone is for it to be considered a value important enough that it ought to be held universally (although not necessarily absolutely or timelessly). We may disagree about what moral values there ought to be—and of course in many societies that disagreement is, to put it mildly, robust. However, such disagreement is not a disagreement about how universal a moral value should be. It is not a disagreement about whether moral values are universal or relative. Instead, it is a disagreement about *which* values should apply universally. (Or, at other times, it is a disagreement about how strongly to weigh those values against one another, or about which values are relevant to a given situation.)

So far, we have looked into the questions of what a moral value is and how there can be a practice that deals in values that apply across all practices. We have not asked the more vexed question of which values ought to be the universal ones. And, in fact, we won't ask it. To try to answer the question of which values ought to be the universal ones is to try to construct a general moral theory. That (thank goodness) is not the task of this book. Since I am concerned here with the issue of practices and their relation to who we are, I won't have to tackle the thorny question of which universal values there ought to be. As far as that goes, I can count on the uncontroversial examples of telling the truth and respecting autonomy that I've been using so far to help me get by in discussing morality.

There is, however, an interesting question in the neighborhood, one that is worth considering. It's not the question of which values ought to be the moral ones, but instead the question of why it is that there is often such disagreement about which values ought to be the moral ones. That question, I believe, *does* have something to do with practices, and will give us some insight into the relation between practices and our moral lives. (I don't want to give an involved defense of what I'm going to say here in response to that question. Think of this, instead, as a suggestion for further reflection.)

In the last part of this book, I argued that people's beliefs are tied, largely, to the practices in which they engage. This occurs by way of their involvement in the inferential structures of those practices. Now those inferential structures have to do, first and foremost, with what people *ought* to believe and how they *ought* to proceed under certain circumstances (not with what people believe *is* the case in one situation or another). As we noted earlier, given the inferential structures of a practice, we could not say what people engaged in a particular practice actually believe—but we *could* say what they ought to believe, given the other things that they actually believe. Given, for example, that someone believes that clitoridectomy is oppressive, and given that that person is engaged in the practice of moral theorizing (otherwise, why use the term *oppressive*?), then he or she is committed to believing that clitoridectomy is morally wrong.

The inferential structures of a practice, however, can concern not only what people ought to believe, but also what they ought to do. In other words, some parts of the inferential structures of practices move from beliefs to actions, not just from beliefs to beliefs (as in the clitoridectomy example I just cited). For instance, in science it is generally believed that a scientist's explanations for things ought not to contradict well-established theories, unless the evidence for contradiction is overwhelming. This isn't a description of what scientists in fact do; it is a normative matter constraining both what scientists ought to believe and how they ought to go about setting up experiments and drawing conclusions from them. In the practice of courtroom law, there are certain moves that an opposing lawyer might make that are considered moves to which one ought to object; other moves are not considered objection-worthy. There are also certain kinds of evidence that ought to be considered good evidence for guilt or innocence, and other kinds of evidence that ought to be considered bad or misleading evidence. In at least some of the practices of friendship, it is considered wise to defer to someone's understanding of his or her own motives, unless that self-understanding is proving harmful. This not only preserves the friendship but also respects the intellectual integrity of the friend.

These "oughts" are, of course, connected with (or *are,* depending on how loosely we want to use the term) the "values" of those practices in which they appear: in these examples, the practices of science, law, and friendship. And, as I suggested earlier, the values of a practice are usually tied up, either directly or indirectly, with its goals. All that I have added here to that earlier thought is that those values are tied not only to goals but also to inferential structures. Or, to put the point in another way, inferential structures reflect and contribute to the values and goals of the practices of which they are a part. Practices, then, involve more or less tightly woven networks of goals, values, and inferential structures.

But now, turn for a moment to people who are engaged in one practice or another—that is to say, us. When we are engaged in a practice, what we are caught up in is not only a way of acting toward a goal but also a way of thinking and valuing. It is not only our behavior that is subject to the practice; through the practice's values and inferential structure, our emotions and our intellect are subject to it as well. (This is a suggestion that I made in Chapter 1, when I talked about how practices mold who we are. At this stage, however, I hope that the point is both more nuanced and more compelling than it was then.) This is not to say that our behavior and our emotions and our intellect are blindly led by the practices in which we participate. We have already seen how one can be critical of a practice even while engaged in it. And we must also keep in mind that nobody is engaged in just one practice; it is possible to remove oneself from the throes of engagement in a specific practice and see it from the perspective of another one. However, it remains the case that, given the bond between goals, values, and inferential structure, participating in a practice is something that involves our entire selves, not simply our actions. Practices are matters of who we are, not simply what we do—or better, they are matters in which what we do and who we are become inseparable.

Because of this, the kinds of things that we think are important and worth the recognition of others are often deeply affected by the practices in which we're engaged. After all, if how I think and what I am attached to and what I do are largely matters of those practices in which I take part, then when it comes to what I believe ought to be valued universally, I am likely to try to sort that matter out by bringing to bear the tools—particularly the inferential ones—given to me by those practices. And, given that people are engaged in very different practices, they are likely to come up with some very different answers about what are and are not candidates for universal values.

There is, of course, a very pedestrian thought behind what I've just said: what people think is right depends in large part on how they see things. What I hope this discussion has added to that very pedestrian thought is the depth of consideration that our reflections on practices have given us.

To see the point more clearly, however, let me turn to an example. In the disagreement over the moral acceptability of abortion, we can recognize how participating in different practices has particular effects on the kinds of beliefs that people think ought to be universal. For many in pro-life camp, universal values depend on the will of a Christian deity. The reason for this is obvious. For such people, participating in religious practices forms a central part of who they are. The values associated with those practices are held closely and are thought to be important enough to be universal. On the other side, many pro-choice supporters are not generally as willing to recognize the values associated with certain religious practices as universal. This is not to say that no one among them is religious, but rather that the nonreligious practices in which they participate are more significantly determinative of what ought to be universal values than the religious ones. (There are, of course, people who support the right to abortion on religious grounds, but their take on religion is very different from those prevalent in the pro-life camp. I leave them aside here for the sake of simplicity.) Practices like feminism or friendship, or certain workplace practices that give women decision-making roles, may significantly shape these people's views about what ought to be the relevant universal values regarding abortion.

Some may want to claim here that I have got things backward. I seem to be saying that practices determine which values people believe ought to be the universal ones, that is, the moral ones. But couldn't things happen the other way around? Couldn't people get involved in certain practices because they *already* believe that certain values ought to be universal? In that case, the practice would not be determining the endorsement of the value, but the endorsement of the value would be determining the involvement in the practice.

Sure enough. I don't want to argue that practices determine commitments to universal values in a straightforward fashion. All along, I have resisted the idea that we are blindly determined by the practices in which we participate. Engagement in practices is, as I have emphasized, a two-way street. My point, then, is not that practices determine the commitment to particular universal values, but the slightly weaker point that practices, because they involve our emotions and our intellect as well as our behavior, help to guide and reinforce certain ways of seeing the world and certain values associated with those ways of seeing. This guidance and reinforcement is related not only to the values of the specific practices in which we engage but also to the beliefs about what values ought to be the universal ones, the values by which everyone ought to live. It may well be that the decision to participate in a particular practice is itself guided by someone's preexisting beliefs and commitments. But, on the other hand, practices also help shape beliefs and commitments. (And don't forget that people are plugged into certain practices even before they are old enough to make decisions about what they approve and what they reject.)

At this point, impressed by the diversity of practices among us and by their diverse values, some people might begin to wonder how it is that we can get moral agreement at all. It might be asked, "With all those different values floating around among all those different practices, how do we get any consensus on which ones ought to be the universal values?" Given the direction the discussion has taken, this has become a question worth asking.

I think that there are two sources of answers to that question, one having to do with the limits of diversity and the other having to do with the role that moral theorizing plays in our lives. Let me take a brief look at each of them.

Although practices are indeed diverse, there are things that constrain that diversity. One of those things, although we don't yet know how much constraint it provides, is biology. As I said early on in Chapter 1, it looks as though genetic constraints are not going to turn out to be determinative of who people are in very fine-grained ways: who one is will not be able to be read off of one's genetic code. Yet genetics and biology generally do offer one sort of constraint on the diversity of human practices and values. (In addition, some theorists have argued that having certain values floating around is biologically adaptive—values, for example, that promote interpersonal respect and cooperation.)

Another constraint is practicality. Take the value of truth telling, for instance. Almost every practice—although, I'll admit, not every one—operates more smoothly if it takes truth telling on board as a value. If a participant in a practice can't trust that a fellow participant is telling the truth, coordination among the various aspects of the practice becomes difficult, if not impossible. Imagine, for instance, trying to engage in some of your own work practices without being able to trust that those around you were telling the truth. How could you be sure of what you ought to do, or whether any of the information you were getting in order to do it was right? Truth telling seems to be a necessary component of the smooth functioning of almost any practice, so it can gain a certain universality across practices simply by its pragmatic necessity. (This does not mean that one must tell the truth to everyone all the time in all practices: certain professional ethics actually may encourage misleading behavior or outright falsity in some circumstances. What it means is that there has to be a core of truth telling in order for the practice to function effectively.) And in addition to truth telling, there are other values that generally enhance practices in one way or another, such as respecting the basic autonomy of others.

Biological and practical constraints, then, form two sources of the commonality of certain values; biological constraints limit the range of values, and practical constraints promote certain values across practices. But another source of commonality is moral theorizing itself. From a very young age, we are brought up to engage in the practice of moral theorizing and to apply that practice to other practices in our lives. When our parents ask us things like "How would you feel if that happened to you?" or "How do you think Sally felt about that?" or "Do you think doing that was helpful?" or "Which do you think is more important, helping Johnny do his homework or going with Jimmy for ice cream?" they are inducting us into the practice of moral theorizing. That induction, of course, does not involve the introduction of sophisticated moral theories. But, as I said before, most moral theorizing doesn't involve sophisticated moral theories, even for adults. It involves certain values which are held to be universal (at least by the people doing the theorizing) and entails a reflection on how those values weigh against one another in their bearing on a specific situation. The kinds of questions our parents ask us when we're kids form the basis for those kinds of values and reflections. And, inasmuch as parents pass down more or less the same values to their kids—which is usually the case—there will be some commonality among moral values across the practices of a particular society.

For these reasons, and probably for others as well, the diversity of values afloat in particular societies does not preclude the possibility of core values that can be commonly recognized as applying across the practices of a society. Given the perspective I'm developing here, what one would expect in the case of moral values would be both agreement and disagreement: agreement on certain core values and disagreement on other values as well as on how the core ones should be applied in given situations. And, in fact, that's just what we have in many societies. If, then, we recognize that (1) moral values are values that apply across practices, (2) moral disagreement arises in good part as a result of participation in diverse practices, and (3) there are certain constraints on practices that work to limit disagreement and to foster agreement, then the broad moral situation in which we find our-selves—as well as the outlines of the specific moral situation in which each of us finds him- or herself—becomes more understandable. After all, isn't it one of the central tasks of philosophy to make our situation more comprehensible to us?

CHARACTERS AND ACTS; IDENTITIES AND PRACTICES

Before discussing the relationship between practices and politics—a discussion that, I hope, will reorient at least some of you in your approach to politics—I want to use the perspective we've developed on morality in order to address two issues related to the question of who we are. These issues are probably best addressed at this moment, the first one because it stems directly from the moral perspective we've now got out on the table, and the second one because it will turn out to stem pretty directly from the first. The first issue has to do with the question of the relation between the moral judgment one passes on a person's character and the moral judgment of that person's actions. The second concerns the currently controversial topic of mul-ticulturalism. Looking at these issues will give us a chance both to see some ways in which our exploration of morality can shed light on concerns closer to the ground and to determine how other aspects of the question of who we are look from the perspective of practices.

The first issue is sometimes called the question of the relation between character and act. In moral theorizing, it is often asked whether it is more appropriate to pass moral judgment on a person's character or on that person's actions. Is the person, or the act, morally good or bad? Some folks—philosophers and nonphilosophers—be-lieve that actions should be judged morally good or bad, not people. For them, it is what a person does or the effect of that person's action that matters, not the person behind the act. That is not to say that just *any* kind of character can commit good acts or bad ones. Certain kinds of characters lend themselves to morally good acts, others to morally bad ones. A person of stingy character, for instance, is less likely to help someone in need than is a person of generous character. But for those who want to focus on the act as opposed to the character, what is morally important is not the stinginess of the character but the help that is either given or withheld. And for many who focus on act over character, the judgment of things like stinginess or generosity of character is merely a derivative judgment based upon the actions a person commits or fails to commit. We assign the character of stinginess to someone *because of* the person's failure to help others in need: the judgment of character is simply a summary judgment based on the judgment of specific acts.

For other people, moral judgment primarily should be placed on the character rather than on the act. (I say "primarily" because there is no complete exclusion of act for the character-promoters, just as there is no complete exclusion of character for the act-promoters. It's an issue of where the moral emphasis should lie.) For these people, it is a mistake to focus on actions as if they were divorced from character. Focusing on actions rather than character leads to too dispersed a view of moral life. If we place our attention on acts alone, we tend to see them as isolated instances that have no deep relation to who a person is. Better, from this perspective, to focus on developing the right kind of character. When people develop the right qualities of character, then the right kinds of actions naturally issue from them. A person who is taught to be generous, and who cultivates generosity as a part of his or her character, will help out people in need just as a matter of course, just because it reflects who he or she is. But if we focus on acts as opposed to character, then we are forced to see each act as arising out of nowhere, as unrelated to the person whose act it is. For those who emphasize character, this approach to morality is a strange and inappropriate one.

The disagreement over attending to character or to act has loomed fairly large in philosophical discussions of morality. For at least several centuries now, the focus of moral theorists has been on acts rather than character. Utilitarians, who believe that morality consists of promoting the most overall good, are straightforwardly interested in the consequences of what people do, not in who someone is. The traditional rival to utilitarianism has been deontology, which is more concerned with rights and duties than with consequences. Nevertheless, deontologists too are more interested in acts than in character.

Although some, like the deontologists who follow the eighteenth-century philosopher Immanuel Kant, focus on the intentions behind the act rather than on its consequences, all deontologists ultimately find the source of moral judgment to lie in what is done rather than in the character of the person doing it. They don't spend much theoretical energy thinking about the development or cultivation of particular personal qualities, and when they do, it is not because they believe that moral judgment primarily concerns character. Rather, it is because developing certain character traits raises the probability of performing the right actions, which is where the real seat of moral judgment is located.

In reaction to utilitarians and deontologists, some moral theorists have suggested that we return to the moral ideas of Aristotle, who was much more interested in the kinds of character people should develop than in the kinds of acts they committed. For Aristotle, morality was primarily a matter of cultivating the right personal traits. To be sure, these traits allowed a person to act in the right way toward others and toward the world. But the crucial issue for him, and the one that is most often cited by more recent followers of his thought, was not what one *does* but who one *is*.

This debate among moral philosophers is, of course, not simply an abstract philosophical one. In our everyday judgments, we struggle with the same issue. For friends and close relations, for instance, we often want to distinguish between character and act, particularly when someone we care about does something we believe to be morally wrong. "He's not really a bad person," we say. "What he did just isn't like him." In saying that, we concede the morally problematic nature of whatever it was that he did, but then go on to say that the proper place of moral judgment is on the character—which is not reflective of this particular act—rather than on the act itself. Alternatively, in the cases of people to whom we are less attached, we are generally more willing to focus judgment on acts, or to judge people solely in terms of their acts, and let matters lie there. Evil is as evil does; best not to try to excuse it. (Another, more complex, case would be that of the conservative religious person who, speaking of homosexuality, wants to "condemn the act but not the person." In this case, assuming that the speaker is sincere and not just trying to avoid seeming judgmental, the division between character and act is going to be something like a division between a person's divine character—as given by God—and the behavior that the person exhibits in the temporal world.)

Our current practice of moral theorizing allows for the focus both on character and on act, although I would guess that the emphasis is more on act than on character. The reason I would guess that—and again, it's just a guess—is that appeals to character seem to be stopgap measures once the judgment of acts has already been made in one way or another. Of course, maybe I think that because I hang around with philosophers, who, as I said, form a more act-judging crowd. But even if I'm wrong about the focus on acts, I think we'll agree that moral theorizing does seem to admit of both possibilities.

But now, how would the question of character and act look from the perspective of practices? Is there anything that thinking in terms of practices has to contribute to this debate? I think that there is. From the perspective of practices, who one is (one's character) is largely a matter of the practices in which one engages and the past practices in which one has engaged. For the sake of simplicity, let's leave aside past practices and focus on current ones. As we've seen, how people act and how they think and feel and are oriented toward others—and toward the world—are tied up with their practices. The idea that there is some kind of neat separation between character and act, then, is a dubious one. Yet it is the idea that there *is* a neat separation—or at least a neat enough one—between the two that allows the debate to get off the ground in the first place.

In agreement with those who want to place the moral emphasis on character, we can affirm that our actions are often expressions of who we are. After all, acts are not simply isolated behaviors, but are instead parts of a larger whole—a practice—into which the actors are more or less integrated. (The degree of integration depends, as we've seen, on how involved or alienated someone is from a particular practice, as well as on the other practices in which he or she is also engaged.) That seems to point the way toward an evaluation of character over act. We can, however, flip the coin and see things from the other side. Once we recognize that acts are bound to the practices of which they are a part, then we can say with equal justice that since the act contains the expression of character, it is the act that should be the focus of moral judgment, not the character. Judge the act, and you'll capture what you need of the character.

For my own part (and for reasons that lie outside the context of this book), I think that the emphasis on acts rather than character is probably the better choice for moral judgment. However, the important point here is that the distinction between the two is not nearly as stark as it may seem. When we isolate individuals from their practices, there can seem to be a gulf between who one is and what one does. On the one hand, you have isolated acts with no particular thread of connection running through them. On the other, you have self-contained characters who have no relation to others and only a vague connection to their actions. Once you begin to see both acts and characters as expressions of the engagement in practices, however, these isolations—and the distinctions that are based on them—fall away, and you're left with a more holistic, more integrated view of the matter. From the perspective of practices, then, the ground upon which the moral debate about character and act rests begins to look fairly shaky.

There is a second issue in the neighborhood, though: one that, like the question of character and act, involves disagreement—and even, in the case of this latter issue, acrimony. This second issue is multiculturalism, which might seem, at first glance, to be rather removed from the debate about character and act. If we look at it more closely, however, I think that we'll see some deep affinities between the two issues.

The debate over multiculturalism has been raging for some time on college campuses. Questions surround the legitimacy of Black Studies or Women's Studies programs; the incorporation of African, South American, and Asian literature into required or general education courses; the removal of recognized Western literary masters from the list of authors studied in required courses in favor of a more ethnically balanced canon; and the introduction of lesser-known female cultural contributors alongside better-known male ones—and all of these questions have found their way into prominence in national publications, classrooms, and coffeehouses around the country. Probably no single issue has so divided university educators as the issue of multiculturalism and the role of a multicultural approach to college and university education.

One way to read the current controversy about multiculturalism—and I think it's the best way—is as a controversy about the extent to which ethnicity and gender can be called forms of identity. In other words, those who favor increasing multicultural awareness and education clash with those who don't over the question of whether we should acknowledge and/or promote ethnic and gender identity as a significant component of who one is. (Notice here that it's possible to acknowledge the identity as a significant component without wanting to promote it, and vice versa. Most people line up, however, answering either *yes* or *no* to both questions.)

Put that way, we can begin to see how multiculturalism intersects with the issue of character and act. Multiculturalism has to do with the issue of character and with the question of what the legitimate components of character are. For multiculturalists, one cannot (or at least should not) talk about who someone is without recognizing that certain features of the person's environment or heritage, features marked by gender and ethnicity, help to shape that person. For those against multiculturalism, these gender and ethnic features either are (or ought to be) irrelevant. We need to see ourselves as part of a universal culture that does not make such distinctions and whose cultural products ought to be judged as better or worse on the basis of some universal set of standards.

For my part, I am sympathetic to multiculturalism, and I believe that anyone who thinks of practices as important in determining who one is would also be sympathetic to it. That does not mean that I agree with all of the proposals that have been promoted under the banner of multiculturalism. What it does mean is that I think that a multicultural understanding constitutes an important part of being a good citizen of the world, and that it is a legitimate role of colleges and universities to promote it. However, although I am sympathetic to multiculturalism, I find myself entirely unsympathetic to many of its proponents. Before I turn to the role of practices in understanding multiculturalism, then, let me spend a moment on some of the mistaken bases for promoting a multiculturalist perspective.

First, some stage setting. The embrace of multiculturalism arose out of the black consciousness and feminist movements of the late 1960s and the 1970s. These movements recognized that being of African descent or being a woman had negative associations within U.S. (and world) culture at large. It was as though being of African descent or being a woman automatically implied that one was somehow lesser in importance or intelligence or creativity or what have you than a man or than someone of European descent. In response to these negative associations, African Americans and women started trying to develop positive senses of identity based on the common ground shared by members of their respective groups. It is probably worth noting that this strategy was not unique to progressive U.S. movements. For instance, black consciousness was also promoted by Steve Biko in South Africa in the 1970s in the struggle against apartheid.

The trick to developing a positive identity as a group is to find something that is both *positive*—something worth taking pride in— and *common to the group*. In being common to the group, the identity doesn't have to be common to every member of the group. But it does have to be identified with that group in some substantial way. Now, what was most common to the groups of African Americans and women at the time of the development of ethnic and gender pride was, of course, oppression. The underlying motivation for developing a positive group identity was to counter the oppression that women and African Americans faced (and often still face). The problem with using oppression as a basis for group identity, however, is that it is negative. If all a particular group has in common is that it is oppressed, that doesn't give it anything to go on as a source of pride. Alternatively, the practice or practices bound up with seeking to overcome oppression would form a good basis for a positive group identity, as long as that positive group identity is not reducible to the experience of oppression.

How, then, to develop a positive group identity?

The two most common strategies that have been tried strike me as failures. The first one I discussed earlier: the claim that you can't judge other cultures because there are no universal criteria for judgment. The idea here is that since there are no universal criteria for judging other cultures, we must respect them by default. Chronologically, it is the later of the two strategies, and was developed largely within the academic community. The point of that strategy seemed to be to recognize that there are cultural differences among people and to respect those differences by blocking the attempt to evaluate them. Such a strategy must fail, as I argued earlier, because it is self-defeating. Even if it weren't self-defeating, however, it's not clear how it would address the problem we're trying to solve. Telling people to respect the cultural differences of others because they have no basis upon which to judge those differences does not tell anybody *what* those cultural differences are that are supposed to be respected. In the case of African Americans and of women, what we want to know is where to look in order to see the real sources that form a basis for a positive identity.

The second strategy, the older of the two, is probably the more popular one. It is to look for something essential in the group that all of its members share and that gives them something of which they can be proud. For the groups in question, the strategy is to find something essential about "blackness" or "woman" that would be a point of pride. To paraphrase Spike Lee: it's a black (woman) thing. If there turns out to be something special about just being black or being a woman, something in which one could take pride, then that something special could be embraced and set up to counter the negative images of women and African Americans afloat in the contemporary world.

Theorists both in and outside of the academic world have worked diligently to develop views of blackness and of women that would render accessible the essentially positive character of each. I think it's safe, although admittedly still controversial, to say that these attempts haven't worked out. To survey all of the attempts would be beyond our task here, but a quick categorization wouldn't hurt. On the side of blackness, if there is something essential about being black that is positive, something built into the nature of people of color, then it has to be either theological or biological. The paths taken by those who would promote an essential black positivity theologically have been overtly racist against nonblacks, a point that has been recognized by blacks and nonblacks generally. The biological path is a nonstarter. As Kwame Anthony Appiah has pointed out in his profound reflection on African philosophy and Africanness, *In My Father's House,* the genetic evidence of differences between blacks and nonblacks has not been forthcoming. Aside from skin color, there are no common genetic differences between people of black skin as a group and those with skin of another color. In fact, the within-group differences among people of one skin color are greater than the differences between skin color groups.

In the case of women, there are, of course, clear biological differences that distinguish them from men. But do those differences amount to anything that can form a source of positive group identity? Frankly, it's been pretty thin pickings. Of course, one can take pride in childbearing, but that has not been the basis for much theoretical work. This is in part because childbearing is a double-edged sword, theoretically speaking: it can be used to reinforce many of the domestic images of women that feminists are trying to escape just as easily as it can be used to promote a positive identity. Many feminist theorists, particularly in France, who have tried to defend the idea of an essential female identity have therefore turned from the straight biological evidence to more baroque forms of psychoanalysis. Outside of a small academic coterie, however, that strategy has not gained many adherents. Suffice it to say that the program of finding something essential about women as a basis for a positive group identity has foundered.

I believe that there are claims to be made on behalf of the distinctness of African Americans and women, claims that do give a sense of the positivity that these movements of identity have sought. In order to see them, however, we must abandon the idea that they belong solely or naturally to African Americans or to women. Or, to put the point in another way, we have to abandon the idea that they form part of an essential identity. You may have noticed that I have introduced the term *identity* here for the first time in the book. When discussing the question of who we are, I have avoided substituting the word "identity" for "who I am" or "who we are." The reason for this is that the idea of identity seems to imply some kind of static, unchanging character, something natural or essential that cannot be modified, or at least cannot be modified without great difficulty. The idea of identity seems to be linked fairly closely to the idea of nature, as in human nature.

However, if we approach the question of who we are by way of practices, then it becomes clear that much of who we are does not possess that kind of static, unchanging character. Although biology may contribute parts of who we are that are more or less static and unchanging, practices do not. Seeing people in terms of practices does not require that there be some fine-grained conception of human nature to which practices respond. Who we are is not a matter of nature so much as it is of what we do in the context of the social norms in which we do it.

As a result, I have avoided the term identity throughout this book, and have introduced it only to describe positions that do seem to seek something that I have argued is not there to be found.

But then, how can thinking in terms of practices help us? How will it give a sense of positive character (if not identity) to women and to African Americans, who have been saddled with a negative identity— even though a false one—for so long? Well, if we abandon the search for what all women or all African Americans have in common simply by being women or African Americans, and begin to look for significant practices that they have taken major parts in creating or contributing to, then we can begin to address this issue. Such creations and contributions are not far to seek. Let me look at two of them briefly.

First, African Americans have largely developed and shaped what is undeniably the most important musical innovation of the twentieth century: jazz. Although long dismissed as a marginal part of music, jazz is finally coming to be recognized in all of its creative and revolutionary character. And, of course, most of those who developed jazz from its inception in ragtime and blues to its contemporary forms have been African Americans. (If they had not been, it is likely that the significance of jazz as a musical form would have been recognized a long time ago.)

It is no accident, at least historically, that it was African Americans who developed jazz. But neither is it, as some (including, at times, Miles Davis) would argue, necessary that one be of African descent to make an important contribution to jazz. The reason that African Americans were most responsible for its development is that they already had an intimate knowledge of the musical origins of jazz. In particular, blues and gospel were musical forms that nearly all African Americans, and very few non–African Americans, were immersed in from birth. Given the deep and continuing relationships between jazz on the one hand and blues and gospel on the other, the historical happenstance that it was mostly African Americans who developed jazz can be explained as more than an accident but less than a derivation from an essential black character. Moreover, and this is the point of the example, jazz is something important and positive that is part of who many African Americans were (and, to some extent, still are). Many African Americans, particularly in the cities, listened to and felt part of jazz at least up until the late 1960s in much the same way that many white Southerners listened to and felt part of country music. Jazz, along with other practices, can fill the role that theories of black identity unsuccessfully sought to fill. (Whether jazz, at least in the cities, is currently being supplanted by rap is an interesting question that this jazz fan will not pursue further.)

As with African Americans, there are many practices to which women, as a group, have contributed significant elements or developed; these practices can form the basis for a sense of who one is as a woman. Let me pick a less well-known example than jazz, because it illustrates something important that will become clearer in a moment. I want to discuss the Pattern and Decoration (or, as it is sometimes called, P&D) movement in contemporary art. The P&D movement was one of the trends in art that emerged in response to the dead end to which high modernist painting had driven itself. After high modernist abstraction had given way (or naturally led) to minimalism, there seemed nowhere else for art to go. Once one has whittled oneself down to nothing, after all, what is left for one to do, or say, or paint? In response to this dead end, a number of trends appeared that ran counter to the intellectualism of high modernism. Perhaps the most famous is Andy Warhol's Pop Art. But another movement, lesser known but nonetheless significant in its contribution, was P&D. It started from the idea that pattern and decoration had always been associated with women and with craft design—and therefore dismissed as nonserious art. While men were immersed in the heady movement of abstraction, women could be left with the frills of decoration. However, when abstraction exhausted itself, an opening was created for the decoration that had been ignored during much of the twentieth century. Feminist artists took advantage of this opening, and began to promote decoration as well as different patterns associated with craft art as legitimate forms of artistic expression. These forms, along-side other art forms associated with non-Western cultures (and, more recently, the postmodernism of artists such as David Salle and Julian Schnabel), moved to the center of artistic expression, and, although modified, have remained there ever since. A glance at contemporary art, not only by many U.S. artists but also by prominent Europeans such as Sigmar Polke, reveals the adoption of decorative components and other craft elements that would have been roundly denounced during the heyday of abstract art.

One of the striking things about the P&D movement is that it took a particular practice of art that was already associated with women, and changed it from being a devalued form of artistic expression into a valued form. Otherwise put, the P&D movement did not involve the creation of a new practice by women; rather, it reassessed the value of an older practice and integrated it into the mainstream of art. What P&D showed—although it is not the only practice to do so—is that practices associated with groups that have been oppressed are often dismissed precisely because of that association. But the construction of a positive group identity, which is one of the important tasks in struggling against oppression, does not require the development of new practices. Instead, it involves the recognition and valuing of practices that have been dismissed or marginalized by the dominant culture.

Although both jazz and the P&D movement arose through the efforts primarily of groups that have been hampered by an association with negative identities, neither of them excludes participation by people who are not members of those groups. Jazz, of course, has had its white participants all along, and recently has gained more wide-spread acceptance among whites. P&D was seized upon not only by female artists but by male artists as well, and has become one of the streams flowing into the larger river of contemporary art. The point of these examples is to show that by abandoning the recourse to some sort of essential identity, and instead turning to practices, one can nourish the needs of marginalized groups for a positive sense of who they are. This is not to say that all people need to participate in the practice, or, in the case of the P&D movement, even be aware of it.

Rather, the participation by large segments of those groups (as in jazz) or the importance of the themes developed in a specific arena (as in P&D) can contribute to the creation of a positive group identity within the group as a whole or in a specific segment of that group (for example, among women artists). And it can be done without having to deal with all of the negative outcomes that movements of identity have brought in their wake.

THINKING ABOUT POLITICS

So far, in this part of the book, we have been looking at the normative role of morality, seeing how moral values are embedded in our daily practices, how the distinct practice of moral theorizing intersects with those other practices, how moral conflicts arise, and how the related issues of character and act and ethnic and gender identity can be better understood through a practice-oriented account of who we are. My hope is that by this point you have become sympathetic to the idea that practices contribute importantly, and perhaps even centrally, to who we are: in a daily way, in our knowledge, and in our values. I'd like to push things a little further before closing, turning to one last way in which looking at ourselves in terms of practices helps us better understand who we are. As with morality, this perspective concerns normative issues. Unlike morality, however, its centerpiece is not so much values as it is power.

So let's have a look at politics from the point of view of practices.

It is a little strange for me to be writing about politics at this moment. As I write this, the U.S. president is about to go on trial in the Senate for lying about having an affair with an intern, many of his accusers are turning out to have had affairs themselves, and the function of government seems to have become to discover who among the opposition is sleeping with whom. If somebody had written a novel delineating the events that are taking place in the nation's capital, no editor would accept it—the plot would be too contrived. In fact, even to mention the word "politics" in decent company—or in any company whatsoever—is to risk ridicule. Politics, it seems, is not for people of vision or integrity or even decency. It's for people who can't, or won't, do any better. One begins to feel about our elected officials in the same way that the comedian Pat Paulsen felt about Richard Nixon years ago. When asked for whom he would vote in the presidential election, Paulsen replied, "Richard Nixon"; when asked why, he said, "I want him where I can see him."

Our elected officials have worked hard to earn the reputation they enjoy today. But one thing they haven't worked for, and it's the thing that I want to discuss, is a certain approach to politics generally, an approach that we need to get past if we're going to see what politics is really about. That approach hinges on the idea that power is essentially something that is possessed by certain (usually large governmental) institutions in a society, restraining what people can or cannot do. Of course, *if* power did work solely by restraining what people can or cannot do, then it would make sense that the larger the institution, the more power it would wield. But if we look from the standpoint of practices, we'll see that power often does not work that way. And, once we see that, we'll begin to see that power is a more subtle and dispersed and creative phenomenon than our traditional view of politics would have it.

Before setting out, I should note that, as with the discussion of knowledge, the view of power that I want to promote is not one I have arrived at on my own. It owes much to other thinkers. It was first—and best—articulated by the French philosopher and historian Michel Foucault. Foucault, whose name is often associated with some of the most unhinged trends in contemporary European philosophy, was, to my mind, a thinker of the first order. Unlike some of his contemporaries, such as Jacques Derrida or Jean Baudrillard, Foucault—at least in his later work—sought not so much to call the entire Enlightenment tradition of reason into question, but to show that there are many forms of reason, not just one, and that there are political consequences that depend on which forms of reason one chooses. When the dust has settled on the skirmishes of late-twentieth-century thought, I think that one body of work that will remain standing is Foucault's.

The view of power that derives from Foucault and that I want to develop is probably best seen against the backdrop of traditional political philosophy. Most of traditional political philosophy, particularly the dominant strain of liberal political philosophy (not to be confused with liberalism as a set of social policies), originated with the British thinker John Locke and the French theorist Jean-Jacques Rousseau. This sort of political philosophy is concerned with issues that exist at a much higher level of generality than that of practices; it addresses concepts such as society and government. Representative questions for traditional political philosophy might be these: What does a just society look like? What are the proper rules by which we would contract with one another to form a society? What are the appropriate functions and limits of government? Where do governmental authority end and individual rights begin? Such questions ask us to think of ourselves as more or less anonymous individuals inhabiting a society whose rules are applicable to all of us and whose power is exercised upon each of us equally.

There is certainly a place for thinking like that. There are, no doubt, political rules that ought to be derived from reflecting on society as a whole or on governmental authority and its limits. But in thinking of ourselves as anonymous individuals, shorn of any particular social engagements, outside of our specific historical and economic and technological environments, a lot is missed as well. And if we begin to assume, as many political philosophers seem to, that the job of political philosophy ends when the general questions of society and government have been answered, then we'll miss a great deal—probably most—of what power is and how it operates in people's lives.

Before turning more specifically to the issue of power, I should pause a moment to call attention to another strain of thought that has also addressed the impersonal nature of much recent political theory. That strain, known as *communitarianism,* argues that much political philosophy has been vitiated by trying to construct a view of justice without taking into account the concrete shape and values of the specific society for which it is prescribing that justice. And theorists like Michael Sandel (in his book *Liberalism and the Limits of Justice*) argue that such an attempt goes wrong in at least two ways. First, by thinking of people as impersonal beings that are substitutable for one another, it misses the contributions that people's contexts make to who they are. Second, it misses the fact that those contexts, including the values that make them up, must always be considered in political theorizing.

It would take a separate book to evaluate the claims of communitarianism in its debate with liberal political philosophy. The debate has become fairly abstract and technical. For the record, I'm not convinced that the critique of liberal political philosophy will hold in as strong a form as communitarians would like. On the other hand, I am sympathetic to their view that a full political reflection does require that we focus on the context of values and beliefs within which people carry out their lives. And although communitarians have not said so, I think that what they are getting at in their discussion of context is the idea of practices. But if we're going to see how to take that reflection forward—at least in a political direction—the proper approach, as Foucault argued, will be to focus on the question of power and its place within our practices.

First let me say a bit about how power will look to us if we only stick with the questions asked by traditional political philosophy, and then I'll turn to how we *ought* to see it. As I mentioned earlier, the traditional approach to political philosophy tempts us to see power as something that is possessed and wielded by social institutions, usually large governmental ones. It also sees power simply as a matter of restraint or repression. Those two ideas of power—as belonging to large institutions and as operating by restraint—are connected. We'll see how by looking a little more closely at the first idea.

If we only ask about the nature or the requirements of a just society or a just government, we tend to ask these questions: "Where should it lie?" and "Who should have power, and how much should they have?" The reason we tend to ask those questions is that questions of justice, asked at a societal or governmental level, tend to be questions of who should get what. In the terms used by political philosophers, the questions tend to be about *distributive* justice, about the distribution of various social goods. This tendency applies to power, just as it applies to rights and other goods.

People worry about where power should lie, about who should have it and how much, because they recognize that if power is abused, it could harm people in unfair or unjust ways. If, for instance, we allow the military institutions of a society to make decisions about the conditions under which—and against whom—to go to war, it would be tempting for the top brass to make decisions that reflect their interests rather than the interests of society as a whole. (And if they made the wrong decision, who would have the means to stop them?) Therefore, it's better to have a civilian in charge of decisions like that, a civilian who is a representative of the general social interest. To put the issue in terms of power, the power of the military (its near monopoly on a society's means of violence) must be checked by the power of civilian oversight (its decision-making authority).

If we look at power in this way, we're assuming that power is something that can be distributed to one institution or another. And the point of a just distribution of power is to make sure that nobody gets too much of it. And the way to ensure that nobody gets too much of it is to have several large governmental institutions in society, each of which has enough power to check the power of the other. That, of course, is the motivation for the creation of the various checks and balances in the U.S. Constitution.

In this approach to political philosophy, then, there is an assumption that power is something that is distributable. There is another assumption about power that is operating here as well. Not only are we assuming that power is something to be distributed to various institutions—usually large ones, since that's where political philosophy focuses its attention; we are also assuming that power works by restraint, by stopping things from happening that, barring the use of power, might otherwise happen. To see how this assumption is also involved, recall the example of who gets decision-making power regarding declarations of war. In that case, the potential power of the military, the one that needs to be limited, is the power to violate the will of the society. It is the power to restrain the members of that society from imposing their will on the general direction that their society—and with it their individual lives—will take. In order to prevent that power from being abused, another kind of power must be set up in order to restrain its operation. That other kind of power is, of course, the one given to a civilian decision maker, who has power over the military precisely to the extent that he or she can restrain the military from making decisions about when and against whom to go to war.

The way power operates, when you're using this distributive model, is by stopping one or another institution (or individual) from doing something. The reason to stop it is, of course, that allowing it to operate unchecked could lead to an injustice. Nevertheless, it is by stopping something or someone, by restraining or checking, that power is seen to work. The assumption that power is something distributed to large institutions, then, is inseparable from the view that power operates by repression or restraint.

This view of power is fine, as far as it goes. And, in fact, in creating and sustaining the democratic institutions of a society, it goes pretty far. Unfortunately, however, it does not go very far in recognizing the various forms of power that operate in people's concrete lives. As I have noted, looking at power at this level of generality assumes that people are anonymous and interchangeable individuals without specific social, technological, and environmental contexts within which they carry out their lives. You can readily see why. The approach to power that liberal political philosophy takes is made at such a high level of generality that it is supposed to be applicable to societies regardless of their specific practices or contexts. For traditional political philosophy, a just society has particular distributions of power with their particular checks and balances, and those distributions and those checks and balances hold for all societies, whatever their history and current social arrangements. Or, to be more exact, they hold at least for all societies that have general ideas about justice that resemble ours.

We need, then, to expand our view of power to include not only the *restraining* power of large institutions but also the *constraining* power of the daily practices in which we are immersed. The idea of constraint (as opposed to restraint) involves not only the act of repression but also the creative act of making something, of forming it. Constraint is not simply the power of prohibition, the power of *no;* it is also the power of producing something that wasn't there before. One restrains someone *from* doing something, but one can constrain someone *to* do, or even be, something.

To see how power constrains our lives, we need to turn back to the workings of practices and to pull together a few of the threads from our discussion of practices so far. In the first chapter of the book, we saw that practices informed who we were both by involving us in certain, often cooperatively approached, goals and by molding our behavior. In the second chapter, we saw that the kinds of things we believe are not simply up to us as isolated individuals, but depend on the kinds of inferential practices in which we are immersed. In the first sections of the current chapter, we saw that our values—moral and otherwise—are bound to the kinds of practices in which we participate, or at least those we endorse. And who we are—what we do, what we believe, what we feel—is being created and sustained by the practices in which we engage. To be sure, we have some say in how that creation goes. As we saw earlier, practices can be criticized and changed either internally or by means of other practices. Nevertheless, our practices go a long way toward making us who we are.

And they do so not so much by restraining us, by stopping us from doing things we might otherwise do. Instead, they do it by forming us, by creating us to be the kinds of people we are. By being immersed in certain inferential patterns, for instance, we are not simply *prevented* from thinking in certain ways; we are taught *how to* think in certain ways. We are immersed in specific patterns of reasoning that, to a greater or lesser extent, become our own patterns of reasoning. It's hard to see how it could be otherwise. People can't learn how to reason without some kinds of inferential patterns in which to be immersed. Although we may be born with the ability to reason—and perhaps even with some primitive tendencies to reason in certain ways and not in others—engaging in the specific kinds of reasoning that people do in their societies requires much more finely tuned inferential patterns than those provided to us by nature or those we can think up all by ourselves.

What holds for inference and belief also holds for values. It is entirely possible that people are born with certain sympathies toward others and with aversions and attractions to certain kinds of behaviors, and that these sympathies, aversions, and attractions contribute to the kinds of values that people have. But these innate tendencies, to the extent that they exist, cannot explain the specific values, moral and otherwise, that people will hold as they get older. In order to explain those values, we have to understand the practices to which they have been exposed and in which they have engaged. With values, as with inference and belief, who we are is largely a matter of our practices.

The first lesson to draw from all this is that who we are is *con*-strained by our practices, not merely *re*strained by them. Who we are, as well as who we are not, derives significantly from our practices. That should not be a controversial claim by this point. We've been looking throughout the book at how practices form us; right now I'm just attaching a little bit of new vocabulary ("constraint," "restraint") to the same phenomena I've been discussing all along. The second lesson, which *is* news, is that those constraints should be thought of as matters of power.

Think for a moment about why power is an issue for us in thinking politically. (And by "us," I mean not just political philosophers but all of us.) Power has to do with who one can and cannot be and what one can and cannot do. To have power over people is to be able to get them either to be or not to be something, or to be able to get them to do or not to do something. Politics is inseparable from the idea of power, and power is inseparable from the idea of constraint. Although traditional political philosophers have focused their energies on the not-doing and not-being part, we all recognize that what is at stake in power are doings and beings as well as not-doings and not-beings. It all has to do with the kinds of control to which we are subject.

Although we all recognize this, the reason that many political philosophers have often neither seen nor addressed it is that their reflections take place at a very general level—at the level of society or of large institutions. However, the power that does not simply restrain us but also creates us is located at a much more local level—at the level of practices. When we turn our attention from the question of what a just society or a just government is—with its assumption that power is a matter of restraint—and toward the question of what makes us do and be certain things, then we can begin to see our way clear to a more nuanced understanding of power.

When we look at power in this way, not only do we see that power is creative as well as restraining. We also see that power is often not the possession of any particular institution or person. Recall here that I said that the dominant approach to political philosophy had two interconnected assumptions: that power is a possession of particular institutions and that it is repressive or restraining. We have seen how the second assumption doesn't really work. Since the two assumptions are connected, it isn't surprising that the first assumption doesn't work either.

From a practice-oriented view, there isn't necessarily any person or any institution that is forming us or creating us or turning us into what we are becoming through our participation in those practices. The values, inferential patterns, goals, rules, non-rule norms, and so on that constitute practices and that contribute to who we are are not the product of some institution (governmental or otherwise) deciding that we ought to be certain kinds of persons and not others. Instead, the character of a practice develops and changes in a variety of ways: by responding to changing environments, by facing criticism either internally or through another practice, by interacting with other practices, and the like. Although it might be possible in some very unusual circumstances to find a practice that constrains people in certain ways because some institution associated with that practice has designed it that way, such a situation is going to be very much the exception, not the rule. As far as practices go, any kind of conspiracy theory about how people become who they are is going to be wildly implausible.

To sum up, then: just as the view that power acts by repression or restraint is inadequate, so too is the view that power is the possession of or can be distributed to one social institution or another.

Faced with this new view of power, one might want to ask, "What would be the political point of seeing power in this wider sense? Why look at power as involving not only restraints but constraints as well? How does that contribute to our political thinking or to political philosophy?" Granted, we do treat power in this way, even if we don't explicitly theorize it as such. But what do we gain when we reflect upon our political situation by embracing this view of power?

This is an important question, particularly for someone like me, who wants to think in terms of practices. After all, another way to put the question would be to say, "How does this new view of power contribute to the goal of the practice of political philosophy?" Put in that way, the question asks me to justify the view of power I'm promoting here within the framework of thinking about our goals and our behaviors that I have been building and defending up to this point.

In order to see how this new view of power can contribute to our philosophizing about politics, we need to have in front of us the goal of such philosophizing in the first place. The point of political philosophizing is not, first and foremost, to give a *description* or *explanation* of how society works or how a political system works or how power works. Political philosophizing is not primarily a descriptive or explanatory endeavor. It is primarily a *normative* endeavor. In political philosophizing, we ask about society, government, power, and related phenomena in order to get a sense of how arrangements of power ought to happen, how society ought to be ordered, how government ought to function. In short, political philosophizing is a matter of values rather than of explanation.

If we ask about how arrangements of power ought to happen, how society ought to be ordered, how government ought to function, and so on, we do so because we want to know which kinds of interventions into people's lives are ultimately acceptable and which kinds are unacceptable. We want to get a sense of how people ought and ought not to be treated by the institutions and within the practices of their society. When and how is it okay for people's lives to be impinged upon in certain ways? When and how is it not okay?

So political philosophizing is a lot like morality: they both concern obligations toward our fellow human beings (and often nonhuman beings). The difference between morality and political philosophy— if there really is a difference worth noting—is that morality tends to focus on individual obligations and individual situations, while political philosophy tends to focus on larger collectives. (Of course, given the view of power that I'm outlining here—where power arises largely in practices—that difference can be a pretty elusive one.)

But now, if the goal of political philosophizing is the normative one of judging acceptable and unacceptable interventions into and impingements on people's lives, then in order to meet that goal, we also need to understand what those interventions and impingements are—the ones that constrain us as well as the ones that restrain us. It won't do to have a political philosophy that says that people can be made into anything you like, as long as thus-and-such particular restraints are built into the social arrangement of society. To take that stance is to refuse to look at the many interventions and impingements that affect people's lives. It is to turn a blind eye to the workings of power. Suppose, for instance, that there was a society that had a large number of practices of which the effect (although perhaps not the goal) was to turn people into timid, unforthcoming, unthinkingly obedient automatons. Would we really want to say that the only point of political philosophizing for that society would be to articulate what the institutional limits and restraints ought to be? Of course not. A proper political reflection would also be to ask whether the practices themselves were acceptable, whether the constraints that they created for people were reasonable constraints for practices to produce. And inasmuch as that kind of question becomes an appropriate political question—and, given the goal of political philosophizing, it certainly seems to be—then we must widen our concept of power to include not only the restraints or limits that power imposes but the things it creates or molds as well.

This new view of power (and the widened task of reflection that it implies) does make the business of political philosophizing more complicated, and it raises some interesting questions about how to evaluate power. I want to return to some of those questions in a bit. But before that, it's probably worth pausing over this new view of power and its place in practices to see how it might look more concretely. So far, we have remained at a general level in our discussion of power. We have talked about power and practices without looking at examples of how power might work in the context of practices. What I want to do now is to draw on one of Michel Foucault's specific analyses of power in order to show, in a concrete way, how politics looks from the perspective of practices. Carefully examining this analysis will, I hope, help put some flesh on the skeleton of abstraction that we have been constructing so far. And it will allow us to pose some challenges that will help to deepen our understanding of the relation between practices and power.

SEX, PRACTICES, AND POWER

The example I want to use comes from the first volume of a proposed six-volume study entitled *The History of Sexuality*. Foucault died while writing the fourth volume, so only three volumes have been published. What's more, after writing the first, he found that the second and third volumes broke with it, taking him into some new and unexpected directions. So the first volume of the series, the one we're going to consider, turns out to be a pretty freestanding work. It's a sketch, an overview, designed for a much larger work that—inasmuch as it exists at all—turned out very differently from the way in which it was originally envisioned. Nevertheless, that sketch offers a good example of how power works in the context of practices, and therefore of what politics would look like from the perspective of the specificity of our lives rather than from the general level of society or of government.

Foucault chose the area of sex as his subject because, among other reasons, he thought that in Western society, we are taught that who we are is a matter largely tied up with sex. In fact, he believed that although sex has been around a long time, the idea of *sexuality* as a distinct strain in people's personalities or as a demarcated group of practices is a fairly recent one. What he set out to discover, then, was how sexuality came about and how it became largely constitutive of who people are.

It is surprising, Foucault wrote, that we live in an age that declares itself one of sexual liberation. (When Foucault published the first volume of *The History of Sexuality* in 1976, the idea of a recent sexual liberation would be even more readily assented to than it is now, over twenty years later.) In fact, he claimed, we have been discoursing about sex incessantly for the past several hundred years. Although the mode of discourse has changed, the fact of discourse has been an intimate constant of our civilization at least since the rise of a certain approach to confession in the Catholic Church. (The term *discourse* here does not only mean talk but also other forms of nonverbal address, as we'll see in a bit.)

Over the course of the seventeenth century, the practice of confession changed. Confession had been a ritual in which one was supposed to admit to behavioral transgressions—sins one had committed—but by the end of the seventeenth century, or early in the eighteenth, it also became imperative to confess sins one hadn't committed but had only imagined. It was desire, not behavior, that became the object of confession. The key to who one is, then, at least from the perspective of Catholicism—which was the dominant approach in France to answering the question of who one is, though its effects could be felt all over Europe and the United States as well—shifted from the external act to the internal desire, and particularly to sexual desire. As far as the Church was concerned, who one is was a matter of what one wants, usually in the sexual sense, and no longer what one does.

Now that injunction to confess who one is, through one's desire, did not lead to a general opening of talk about sex throughout society. In fact, quite the opposite. Sex became something one did not talk about in public. It was too shameful. One confessed it to the priest, since it, like all sins, required confession. But otherwise, it would not be discussed. Sex—as sexuality, as a group of distinct practices, as the key to one's personality—became the shameful secret that was also the secret of who one is. (Original sin goes mental.) The fact that sexuality was not spoken about did not mean that it was not addressed. There was plenty of nonverbal discourse about sex. A whole set of practices—or modifications of existing practices—arose that concerned themselves with sexuality. Although these practices were verbally silent on the subject, they nevertheless kept calling attention to it.

For instance, sexuality made an appearance in practices of architecture and design. Secondary schools were designed to segregate boys from girls in a way they had not done before. Before the late seventeenth century, it had been thought that sex was irrelevant to boys and girls—after all, they were too young to commit sexual acts. As a result, various (although perhaps not all) forms of gender segregation were irrelevant. But once one's desires, and especially one's sexual desires, emerged as the key to who one was, it became necessary to be sexually vigilant toward all age groups. Such architectural and design innovations as the building of internal partitions and all-night illumination were ways of recognizing and regulating the sexual desire that was at the core of who boys and girls—as well as adults—are.

At the same time, changes in the practices of economic and political analysis were leading to a focus on sex from a different direction. The concept of population moved to the center of economic and political analysis as theorists grappled with questions of how manpower would affect a country's economic, military, and political standing. Issues such as birth rate, sterility, and the status of marriage started to assume more importance in studies of political economy. And, of course, as population became more of a concern, so did sex. There was a convergence, then, of theories—religious theories and those based on political economy—on the importance of sex. Sex, once a set of acts, now began to emerge as an expression of who one was and what one's proper place in society was. Sex was becoming what Foucault called "sexuality."

Over the course of the late eighteenth century and into the nineteenth, medicine got into the act. Studies of children's sexuality, the sexuality of "criminals" and "perverts," homosexuality, and the sexuality of women became central to medical research. Both reinforcing and reinforced by these new studies, health professionals observed increasing numbers of people in Europe and intervened in their sexual lives. The secret of sexuality was afloat, and this secret had to be revealed constantly to the experts—religious, medical, economic, and public health experts—in order to assess the state of one's soul and the health of one's society.

From this perspective, the emergence of psychoanalysis in the late nineteenth and early twentieth century was not so much a break with past practice as it was an extension of it. Freud may have revealed the Great Secret, but in doing so he buttressed both its importance in constructing who one is and the confessional mode by which that construction is reinforced.

This is just a quick summary of Foucault's history, but I want to use it not so much to make his case for him as to show how a politics of practices would look. I would like to linger over some implications of this sort of history. But before discussing those implications, let me point out a few of its notable aspects. First, what Foucault has offered here is a history of practices. He has neither told us how society should look nor told us how government ought to work. And he has said very little about how government does, in fact, work, except in some specific policy functions regarding public health. What we have instead is a history of the convergence of several practices in a specific area, and their creation of an object of study in that area.

Second, the new object of study that is created—sexuality—has political consequences, as long as we think of power as constraining and not merely restraining. Inasmuch as people are subject to the emerging concern with sex within various practices, they are being turned into beings of certain kinds of sexuality. We have seen throughout this book how the participation in a practice helps to make one who one is. In the case study that we're currently considering, it is not merely one practice but several that are in play and converging. Imagine getting the same message about who you are from your priest, pastor, or other religious guide, your medical doctor, your psychiatrist or psychologist, and the talking heads on television or in the newspapers. The message, repeated enough from enough different angles, has an effect. This does not mean, of course, that it cannot be resisted. It can. But resistance is difficult, and for the most part it will not happen. There is also a cost for resistance, give our particular social arrangements. The resister is labeled by the experts as "abnormal" or "perverse"; therefore, the resister's message takes on the taint of an inferior sexuality.

What is happening here, then, is not so much the *restraint* of sexuality as its *constraint*. It's not as though there were some natural sexuality that people otherwise might have had and that is being blocked or obstructed by the emerging practices of sexuality. Rather, people's sexuality is being created; who they are is, in important ways, being constructed for them. This is not, of course, to say that people wouldn't have sex if it were not for these practices. People had sex before these practices arose, and will have sex after they fade away. Rather, the coalescing of sex into sexuality and the emergence of sexuality as the secret of who one is are being created for them. People have become, in new ways, sexual beings.

Foucault discusses some of the ways in which people were created to be who they are during the historical rise of the practice and discourse of sexuality. He points to several "figures" who emerge over the course of this period; for him, "figures" are images of people that more or less closely correspond to who people are becoming. These figures are new in Western history. One of them is the masturbating child, a figure who is preoccupied by sexual thoughts, is always ready to enact them, and must be constantly monitored by parents, teachers, and public health officials. Another is the Malthusian couple, spouses who see the dangers of their sexuality and are at pains to harness it only to the benefit of the larger social (and theological) whole. Those of you familiar with the constrictions and restrictions regarding sex associated with the bourgeoisie during the Victorian period will immediately grasp the importance of this particular figure. The masturbating child and the Malthusian couple were among the figures helping to create and reinforce certain ways in which people behaved, thought, and felt during the period of sexuality's ascendancy as the Great Secret of who one is.

Stepping back from the example of sexuality, we can see that looking at the level of practices—rather than at the more general level of society or government—allows us to begin to grasp how subtly power can work in directing people's lives. We might have missed those subtleties if we had kept our attention focused on the more general level. Again, this does not mean that we ought to abandon the general level for the specific one. What we should do instead is bear in mind, even as we try to answer the broad questions that much of political philosophy puts before us, that there is always much more to politics and therefore to political theory. (And that "more" part might affect the answers we give to the broad political questions.) We need to be vigilant about how power is not only *restraining* us from acting in certain ways but also *constraining* us to act in certain ways. And to see the constraints, we need to reflect on the power mechanisms at play in a society's practices.

We can also see another important theme in Foucault's writing, one that I have not yet mentioned but that deepens our view of the social role of practices. In defining a practice, I said that most practices have goals. They have ends in view that the participants in that practice are trying to achieve. What this example shows, however, is that practices can have effects that are distinctly different from their goals. In other words, we should not define the social consequences of a practice simply by the goals it posits for itself (or, more accurately, the goals posited by its participants). We need to look, as well, at the interaction of the practice with other practices and institutions in society and to assess the consequences of those interactions. Drawing an example from the case at hand: it was not the goal of economic analysis, when it turned to population studies, to create a new sense of who people were. The goal of economic analysis was to understand how wealth was created and how it could be maximized. One of its effects, however, was to assist in the creation of the Malthusian couple. This figure did not originate solely within the practice of economic analysis, of course, but resulted from the interaction of economic analysis with contemporary theological, medical, and public health practices. The effects of economic analysis, in its interplay with other practices at the time, outran the goals that it had set for itself.

We can see this idea at work in our current society as well. As I'll address in detail in the next section, one of the effects of the pervasiveness of electronic media in contemporary Western society is that people have become more isolated from one another. Because we can watch movies at home instead of having to go to a movie house, because we can find out the news without having to walk out to a newsstand or any other public space, because we can have virtual experiences of other places without having to travel to them, and because many of us can contact people by e-mail without having to see or even hear them, the social world most of us inhabit has diminished in scope and vibrancy. Now, it is hardly the intention of those engaged in the practices of computer and electronic research and development to isolate us from one another. The goals of such practices, as far as I can tell, have to do with making life more convenient, seeing what technology can accomplish, and making money for their participants. It would certainly be stretching a point to say that one of the goals of computer and electronic research is to ensure that people's lives become more isolated from public space. (In fact, one could argue that those engaged in developing and refining e-mail hope to enlarge the range of public space: e-mail, the argument would go, allows us to contact increasing numbers of other people who might share our interests but who might live quite far away. And, in fact, e-mail *does* accomplish that. But I believe that it does so at the cost of deeper personal isolation.) So, inasmuch as our public space—the space we share with one another, willingly or unwillingly—has shrunk, and inasmuch as that shrinkage has had to do with (but not solely with) the development of electronic media, there are practices afloat in our society that have had effects distinct from, and perhaps even contrary to, the goals the participants in those practices have had in view.

So far in this section, we've looked at an example of how power functions at the level of practices in helping to make us who we are, and have seen that the effects of practices can diverge from their goals. We might want to return at this point to the question of why it would be important to study politics at the level of practices—and in the light of the example, we will come to a more concrete answer to that question.

I earlier raised the question of why it is worth recognizing the existence of power at the level of practices. My answer then was that since the goal of political reflection is the normative one of asking about the acceptability and unacceptability of certain power arrangements, it is important to know how power is restraining and constraining people at all levels, not merely at the level of government or society as a whole. Foucault's example of sexuality helps us see why. Given the history that he has put before us, we can now question the acceptability of the practices—or of certain aspects of the practices—that, among other things, constrain our sex lives along some particularly narrow pathways. Is it acceptable to engage in practices that perpetually monitor children? Should we accept the Malthusian couple as the only appropriate sexual arrangement? Should we label and condemn those whose sexuality does not fall within the sexual norms that have gradually come to govern our society over the past several hundred years? And behind all these questions, another one: should we really think of sexuality as important to who we are? These political questions are ones that we are able to ask once we start to recognize that power functions at the level of practices, and that it contributes to who we are and to how our lives go just as much as, and in some cases more than, its functioning at the level of government or of large institutions. They are the kinds of questions that concern what happens to us and who we become. They are questions of power—of the constraints that our social environment places upon us. They are also questions that can be answered only by looking at the practices in which we are involved and at the interaction among those practices.

Before closing this section, there is one more question that we need to consider. It is a challenge that often confronts the kind of political viewpoint we've been developing here. Although the answer to this question is fairly complex, I think that a quick overview of how it might go would usefully deepen our understanding of the role that political reflection plays in thinking about our lives.

The question arises from the recognition that if power exists at the level of practices, then it is pervasive in our lives. After all, we're no longer talking about whom the government can and can't lock up, or the conditions under which the military can be brought into play, or whether the government ought to be able to tax people with large incomes in order to help people with small or no incomes. We're talking about things that happen to us and things that we do every day: if I've been right up to this point, we're talking about some of the most central aspects of who we are. But if power is that pervasive, if it affects all practices, then how are we to judge which practices (or which aspects of which practices) are acceptable and which are unacceptable? Won't any judgment itself come from a practice that has its own power arrangements? Won't acceptability and unacceptability just be matters of different powers competing against one another for dominance? Won't judgment about "better" and "worse" just resolve itself into an issue of which practice can impose its values on others? And if so, won't the idea of "most acceptable" ultimately be the same thing as the idea of "most powerful"?

People often try to dress up one kind of power play or another in moral garb, lending it that particular kind of righteous sheen that only morality can give. But if all practices are merely power plays, then whatever practice is supposed to do the normative evaluation of another one—whether it's the practice of morality or some other practice—is itself only a player in the game of power. There isn't really any kind of evaluative judgment. Instead, there are only certain power moves that dress themselves up as normative evaluations.

In responding to this worry, what we need to get clear on is that the idea that power is every*where* does not imply that power is every-*thing*. I'm prepared to admit that power exists in all practices (or at least in any practices that I can imagine). And I'll admit that power is constantly constraining us to be certain kinds of people. It does not follow from that admission, however, that all there is to practices is power.

Suppose, for instance, that I say that sexuality ought not to be considered some sort of Great Secret in our attempts to understand who people are, and I back up that claim with the justification that regarding sexuality as a Great Secret unnecessarily constricts not only people's sexual lives but also their general ability to create themselves as they see fit. In short, it violates their right to autonomy. In that case, I'm speaking out of a practice of—or at least a practice that involves—normative evaluation. Most likely I'm speaking out of the practice of morality. (In order to be sure that the practice out of which I'm speaking is morality and not some similar practice, we'd probably have to look a little more deeply into my specific reasoning. But we don't need to know that in order to address the issue at hand.) Now suppose further that my idea comes to seem generally justified, and that we change our practices so that sexuality no longer seems to be the Great Secret. Suppose, in fact, that it comes to be believed that there is no Great Secret to who anybody is, and that people are mostly formed by the practices in which they engage over the course of their lives. (A formidable idea.) If all that happens, my evaluative judgment has contributed to a change in how people see themselves, a change that certainly will have its own constraints. So my judgment has had effects of power. The question is whether that judgment is nothing more than a matter of power.

It seems pretty clear to me that, while it is a matter of power, it is not *only* a matter of power. It is also, among other things, a matter of justification. It is a matter of having certain practices of power con- form to our idea of justified, rather than unjustified, practices of power. If the idea of people's being who they are as a result of the practices in which they engage is better justified (both as a better explanation and, normatively, as an idea that allows them more au- tonomy) than the idea of people's being who they are as a result of the secret of their sexuality, then the constraints of the practice-oriented view will be justified constraints, while the constraints of the sexuality-oriented view will not.

This may not seem to be enough to answer the question. Somebody could come back and say that while it is true that some forms of power are justified relative to certain practices, and others not, those practices themselves (the ones doing the judging), *including* their justifications, are just matters of power. My response to this further objection is that while all justified evaluative judgments may be matters of power, not all matters of power can be evaluatively justified. There are forms of power that can be evaluatively justified, and forms that cannot be. For example, forms of power exercised to restrain people from harming innocent others can surely be justified, while forms of power whose effects are to prevent consenting adults from expressing affection toward one another cannot. And if we turn to the justifications themselves, we can ask the same question of whether the power constraints that arise from those evaluative judgments are themselves justified relative to some further evaluative criteria.

But here the questioner may seem to have won. At this point, she or he can say, "Aha. If you admit that even the evaluative judgments are constraining, then no matter how far back you go—evaluating the evaluations, evaluating the evaluations of those evaluations, etc.— you'll always have power operating." Agreed. But that doesn't clinch the point for the questioner. My claim is *not* that you won't have power operating no matter how far back you go. You will. My claim is that in addition to power, you also have justification. Or, to put the point in another, more accurate, way: even when justification involves power, it isn't reducible *to* power, because some power constraints are justified and others are not. So although all evaluative justification may involve power, we can't say that justification equals power. Some constraints of power are justified, others not. To repeat: even though power is everywhere, it is not everything.

What the questioner may be looking for here in order to settle the issue once and for all is some form of evaluation that does not involve power, some form of evaluation that can stand outside all forms of power in order to be able to pass judgment upon acceptable and unacceptable forms of power. But if all practices involve power, then in order to be able to stand outside of all forms of power, this kind of judgment would have to be able to stand outside of all of our practices as well. In the terms we used earlier in the book, it would have to be some sort of foundationalist judgment. But if the idea of foundationalism is suspect, then so is the idea that power can be judged from outside power. The point that I have been promoting here is that although all evaluative judgment involves power, this does not mean that we have to concede that evaluative judgment is nothing more than power. Such judgment involves power, but it isn't simply a form of power.

So far in this chapter I have been looking at morality and politics through the lens of practices. If we add the developments here to the previous arguments about practices, we come up with a pretty comprehensive picture of ourselves and our lives. However, it is not the only picture we might create. Before closing, then, we should spend a few minutes looking at competing theories of who we are, and one competing theory in particular, to see how their visions differ from the one I have been defending here.

CONCLUSION: THE END OF PRACTICES?

For some years, I have talked about practices and the role they play in our lives before a number of audiences (though, fortunately for them, not at this length). The response has been pretty encouraging. People seem to think that there is something to the idea that looking at ourselves through the lens of our practices allows us to see who we are more clearly than does looking through other lenses. But during those talks, a particular kind of question has often arisen—and I wasn't at first entirely clear on its motivation. As I seemed to get the same kind of question over and over, however, I thought about it more. The more I thought about it, the more interesting it became, and the more it opened up for me.

The question, although it was asked in many different ways, was more or less this: "What might disprove the idea that looking at ourselves through the lens of practices is the most fruitful way in which to see ourselves?" Or put in another way: "What kinds of considerations would work as counterevidence to the framework you're trying to build?" Or yet again: "What would get you to abandon the perspective of practices as a useful one within which to see ourselves?"

At first, the question seemed to me to be about competing views. What views compete against this perspective, and what would tell in favor of another view over that of practices? And, in fact, the question *is* one about competing views. But it is also a question about the state of our world. Is the state of our world such that the perspective of practices fits it well in our attempt to answer the question of who we are?

These two ways of reading the question are related. If the perspective of practices provides a good lens by which to see ourselves, then inasmuch as another perspective is competing with it, there would be reason to pick the perspective of practices over that other perspective. On the other hand, if the perspective of practices doesn't do such a good job, that would be a point in favor of some competing perspective. And if a competing perspective does a better job of telling us who we are, then that argues that the practices perspective may not fit the current state of the world nearly as well. (Recall that, as I admitted in Chapter 1, I don't think of practices as constituting the *whole* answer to who we are. Things like genetics count too. I just think that it constitutes one of the most important perspectives—if not the most important—and one of the most overlooked.)

As I thought more about the question, I began to ask myself what kinds of competing perspectives might, given the current state of the world, give practices a run for their money. Generally, the type of perspective that most often arose was one that emphasized a single explanatory feature to which other features of our world could be reduced. Let me unfold this a bit. Theorists often try to tell us who we are by reference to a single explanatory feature, a single explainer, that takes the complexity of the world and accounts for it as some sort of derivation from that single explainer. Freud thought that we could be explained as products of our unconscious workings. Marx, at least on some readings, thought that who we are could be explained by reference to the economic relations obtaining in our society. Some fundamentalist theologians think that we can be explained by reference to Biblical or Koranic or Talmudic or Vedic doctrine.

The perspective of practices resists this kind of reducing of things to a single explainer. It might look at first as though it doesn't, as though I'm saying something like "It's the practices, stupid," just as Marx (and supporters of Bill Clinton's first presidential campaign) said, "It's the economy, stupid." But the concept of practices doesn't work in the same way at all. For Marx—at least the Marx of this specific reading— you can explain people's politics, their religion, their family structures, and the like all by reference to the economic relations holding in a particular society at a particular time. In the jargon of this kind of reductionism, the economy is the substructure and everything else is the superstructure built on top of it. The same goes for Freud. Civilization, monotheism, you name it—they're all products of the unconscious resolution (or lack thereof) of the Oedipal conflict.

It's not like that with practices. If you want to know how religion works and what it has to do with who we are, you have to look at religious practices, and look at the practices with which religion interacts. If you want to know what families are all about, you have to look at familial practices and the practices with which they intersect. For politics, of course, you have to look everywhere. Unlike the single explainer theory, the perspective of practices does not tell us *what it is* that we have to look at in order to understand ourselves and our world. It tells us *what level to look at* in order to see these things correctly. Don't opt for a perspective that's too large—society as a whole, knowledge as a whole, the cosmos as a whole. Don't opt for one that's too small, either—the individual as distinct from his or her social involvements. Instead, look at the various points at which people intersect with their societies and the norms afloat in those societies: look at their practices. The perspective of practices does not give us an object to look at so much as it gives us a way of looking at a network of objects. It is a *how*, not a *what* or a *where*.

The question, then, changes: "Is there a reductive view of who we are—a single explainer—that is better than the practices view?" In some ways, it would be comforting to have one. A single explainer view has the virtue of simplicity that the practices approach lacks. The practices approach requires us to look at our society's specific practices and their norms in order to understand who we are. That's a lot of looking. A single explainer view only requires us to look in one place:

the economy, the unconscious, the Bible, wherever. We have some motivation, then, at least from the point of view of theoretical simplicity, to look for a single explainer. I take it that psychoanalysis, Marxism, and fundamentalism won't do: they have deep enough problems that they are not currently ready to fulfill the role of single explainer (which is not to say that they don't explain anything, only that they aren't really in contention to do the large job required of a single explainer). Is there anything better out there?

At the moment, I don't think there is. However, there is something on the horizon that threatens to be a better explainer. Let me christen this alternative *technological capitalism,* and then describe its features, which will be familiar to all of the readers of this book.

We live in a world in which capitalism has gone global in an unprecedented way. This is due, in part, to the development of advanced information technologies, which are themselves largely the product of a technologically advanced capitalism. In any case, even large corporations, which were once mostly national entities that might or might not have operations overseas, have now become transnational entities that do not really have a national home or national allegiances. (The history of this evolution is succinctly summarized in an article by Masao Miyoshi entitled, "A Borderless World? From Colonialism to Transnationalism and the Decline of the Nation-State.") As a result of this transformation, companies without any national bonds are determining the lives—both public and private—of people in one country or another in significant ways. Indeed, they are becoming as important as (if not more important than)the (one hopes elected) policy makers of those countries. Or, to put the point in another way, the kinds of factors that determine how people's lives go are coming less from public deliberation and more from the intervention of transnational corporations. Our public space for debate about what our society should look like is being abandoned in favor of a society that is, increasingly, the product of economic decisions by powerful corporate entities.

This trend has, of course, been fostered by the rise of an ideological commitment to discarding many of the traditional roles of government. People are increasingly willing to let the market decide what used to be decided through public deliberation by elected representatives. Since the demise of Soviet-style communism, the market has come to be seen as the answer for almost every question about how social decisions ought to be made.

Entwined with the unprecedented going-global of capitalism has been the profusion of electronic media. When I was growing up (does this date me?), people used to complain that the proliferation of television sets had dampened interpersonal interaction. Now, with the rise of the Internet and e-mail, and the hundreds of television stations to which many of us have access, it's as though we need not walk out the door to experience the world; the world has—at least virtually—come into our homes. And as a result (to pick up on a point I made earlier), the physical interaction among people is diminishing. People are becoming more isolated. Social space is shrinking.

Both the substitution of corporate for public decision making and the isolation promoted by various media technologies converge on a phenomenon that we might term the *privatization of life*. By that I mean the diminishing of public or social space in favor of much more localized spaces that consist only of oneself (or may include a selected few others). The substitution of corporate for public decision making contributes to the privatization of life by eliminating the space of public deliberation, therefore giving people the (often correct) sense that there is no place in which to express or press their views about what the social world should look like. For example, the rise of malls as a replacement for the marketplace has eliminated one of the most common traditional sites of public discussion. Political, religious, or social speech, whether by soapbox, leaflet, or demonstration, was an integral aspect of the public marketplace. And, since the marketplace was public property, such activities were protected. In contrast, making speeches, handing out leaflets, or demonstrating aren't even permitted at most malls. The public exchange of opinions, which was as much a part of the marketplace as economic exchange, isn't even legal at the "marketplaces" most people now attend.

If substituting corporate for public decision making privatizes life by eliminating social deliberation, the recent profusion of media technologies privatizes it by eliminating social interaction. We are decreasingly in physical contact with our fellow citizens. We see them less (although we may see many images of them), we hear them less, and we share the same space with them less. For an increasing number of people, work and entertainment is done at home. Many offices have emptied out, movie theaters are often replaced by videos we watch at home, books are coming to us without our having to step into bookstores, political organizing is happening over e-mail instead of at meetings, and so on. (You can surely come up with your own additions to this list.) For many of us, the world we inhabit is becoming more a matter of screens, usually screens in our homes, and less a matter of the weaving of our lives into those of others.

I am, of course, not the first person to remark on the recent decline in our public and social space. As we saw in the first part of the book, Robert Putnam has concerned himself with our increasing isolation from one another. For Putnam, the loss of participation in civil society has caused this isolation, and it is largely the watching of television that has caused the loss of participation in civil society. Given my sketch here, you can see that I'm sympathetic to his concerns. If, however, we think of watching television as the primary cause of our isolation, without seeing the wider context within which the centrality of television to people's lives occurs, then I suspect that we will misread the real causes of our isolation. It is easy—and not entirely off the mark—to blame people for sitting in front of the television rather than contributing to the maintenance of a vital public space. However, it's not as though there aren't any pressures other than television that are moving us toward an increasing isolation from one another. My claim here is that those pressures are coming from the dominance of a technological capitalism that is increasingly determining the shape of our (and many other) societies.

In addition to Putnam, many political writers—on the left and the right—have addressed these issues. On the left, the tendency is to talk of a loss of community in the wake of technological capitalism, although I don't know whether anybody else uses the phrase "technological capitalism" to describe what I'm getting at here. In keeping with the largely Marxist roots of the twentieth-century left, capitalism has seemed to them to be the primary causal factor—the single explainer—for many of the recent changes in people's lives, especially the polarization of high and low income earners and the growing social isolation. I haven't addressed the issue of polarization, but you can see that I am in accord with this leftist view regarding social isolation. Although I would not ratify many of the specific analyses offered by people who see themselves as being "leftist" or "progressive" thinkers (and who among us on the left ever agrees with anyone else on the left?), I do think that the broad thrust of the left's approach to this issue captures something important about the changes in our world.

Thinkers on the right have also noticed our increasing isolation from one another, but they tend to focus their critique less on technological capitalism and more on what they see as a loss of traditional values. It is the loss of a common social commitment to those traditional values, more than anything else, that has isolated us from one another. Although many conservatives treat that loss as a result of too much tolerance for practices, values, and beliefs different from the traditional ones (and therefore oppose multiculturalism in education), others will admit that the impersonal nature of technological capitalism has at least something to do with it.

Although I won't argue for this point, since it would bring us too far afield of the concerns that have motivated this section of the book, I don't believe that our current sense of isolation is caused by a loss of values. However, I do not want to dismiss the idea, either. There is, I think, something right in the concern about a loss of traditional values; I want to spend a moment capturing it and placing it in what seems to me a better context within which to see it.

One of the effects of the rise of technological capitalism has been the narrowing of the ways in which we go about making evaluative judgments. There is a tendency to substitute the values of the market—cost-effectiveness, monetary worth, and the like—for other types of values that are more resistant to translation into economic terms. This phenomenon was noticed by the French thinker Jean-François Lyotard some years back in his book *The Differend*. One way in which to read *The Differend* is as a book about practices (for which he uses the term *genres*). Read in this way, which I'll admit is a bit of a stretch—but only a bit—Lyotard can be seen as making the case, near the end of the book, that capitalism has tried to reduce all practices/genres into one type, the capitalist type. That capitalist type translates all values into market or exchange values, and all goals to the goal of individuals getting the best exchange for themselves. (It also sees exchange values as ultimately a matter of the exchange of time, but I'll leave that issue aside.) Put into the terms that we have been using, what Lyotard is getting at is that the dominance of technological capitalism has among its most important (and dangerous) effects the reduction of values to marketplace values and the reduction of goals to the goal of personal gain.

I think that we can see the truth of the worry Lyotard places before us in a phenomenon that he doesn't address, one that has begun to emerge forcefully in our society. Who we are is becoming increasingly identified—by ourselves and by others—in terms of our role as consumers. You can see how thinking of oneself largely as a consumer is related to the dominance of technological capitalism. To the extent that values are marketplace values and goals are those of personal gain, then life's point becomes largely a matter of getting the most stuff for the best price. As someone (I don't know who) has said, "He who dies with the most toys wins." It would be a more arduous task than I want to take on here to detail how this thinking of oneself as mostly a consumer manifests itself across society, although I suspect that you can see it around you. To give the idea some flesh, let me use an example from my own life, an example that has been discussed informally by lots of professors, particularly in the humanities.

I have found over the past eight or ten years that many of the students who attend my classes seem to do so, more and more, with a consumerist mentality. They see classes as a form of entertainment for which they have paid, and determine the value of the class as a product of the grades they're given and the entertainment value they've received. As I say this, let me hasten to add that not all students are like this. But this approach to academic life is on the rise. Professors are thought of as entertainers whose job is to keep students awake and give them good grades. What is missing from this way of looking at things is, of course, the value of what might be learned when one engages personally in the material. For students bound to this consumerist mentality, the material is just a bother that has to be got through in order to get the grade and, they hope, a laugh or two out of the course.

If Lyotard's view of the dominance of capitalism, along with my extension of it, is right, then we can see the truth of the conservative worry that we are experiencing a loss of traditional values: many of the values and goals historically associated with the diverse practices of our society are being swallowed by marketplace values and goals. But while the conservative approach wants to see our isolation as resulting from the loss of a common commitment to traditional values, I believe that the loss of values and the isolation *both* result from the dominance of technological capitalism. (There are, of course, some "traditional values," such as the value that all sexual relationships ought to be heterosexual ones, that are better off being lost. But that's another story.)

I have tried here to give you a picture of technological capitalism and its effects. I have not, of course, given you a very detailed picture. Nor have I defended it. Neither detail nor defense has been my point. I suspect that enough of you relate to what I've said that I can get away with using it as a breezily plausible single-explainer alternative to the practices approach to who we are. In essence, what I am considering is the possibility that there is a single explainer for who we are—technological capitalism—currently in evidence throughout our world, one that does a better job of explaining who we are than the practices approach does.

To the degree that the picture I am painting here is an accurate depiction, there are two related and disturbing results for the idea of practices. First, the diversity of practices, with their assorted values and goals, is being threatened. And second, the use of the practices view as an explanation of who we are is diminished. Let me say a bit about each in turn.

The ways in which the diversity of practices is being threatened are fairly straightforward. A single force—technological capitalism—is imposing its goals and values on a variety of practices, thus making them look more alike, that is, reducing their diversity. Moreover, inasmuch as this force is effective in imposing itself across the planet, those practices whose goals and values are resistant to translation into the idiom of technological capitalism will probably find themselves increasingly marginalized, and perhaps even disappear altogether.

Aside from the imposition of a narrower range of goals and values, technological capitalism threatens the diversity of practices in another way. By isolating us from one another through the privatizing of people's lives, it diminishes the social character of life that sustains most practices. Recall that at the outset of this book I defined practices as "socially normatively governed." Not all practices, I said, have to be socially performed—although most are—but they all have norms that are grounded in some form of social life. So what happens when you diminish social life? The source of norms for practices is drained away, and with it the milieu in which most practices are carried out. If the dominance of technological capitalism continues to erode the social character of people's lives, then we can expect to see the emergence of more homogeneous practices and the trivialization of practices—that is, practices coming to seem less vital to people or going by the board altogether.

Let me turn now to the second outcome, one that particularly affects my account of practices, that would result from the dominance of technological capitalism as a single explainer for who we are. For our purposes, this is the more important result, since the issue we're addressing here is whether there are any decent competing theories to the practices approach in answering the question of who we are. So let me offer a quick summary of how an explanation of who we are that sees us through the lens of technological capitalism would go. We are, primarily, economic beings trying to get the best market value for material goods. We are beings whose relation to one another is that of provider to consumer. And this relation of provider to consumer is, most significantly, a competitive one, since each of us is trying to get the best value from all the others. Cooperation exists, but the ultimate goal of cooperation is individual personal gain. In addition, we are rather isolated from one another, in part because of our competitive relation to others and in part because the diffusion of electronic media throughout society has lessened our need for ongoing social interaction and the rise of the mall has blocked the possibility of public deliberation. We are becoming creatures of a largely virtual world that, combined with the amenities that personal wealth has to offer, nestles us in a space of few personal contacts and little public involvement. (Of course, not everybody inhabits such a world. But that is not because they have created a better alternative; it is because, being poor, they are not there yet.)

This, of course, is only a thumbnail sketch of how the question of who we are would be answered by those who think of technological capitalism as an adequate single explainer. It is enough, however, to allow us to see how different we look from that perspective compared with how we look from the practices approach. And it is enough to show us, from the perspective of technological capitalism, how very similar we look to one another. That should not be surprising, since the point of a single-explainer approach is to focus on one particular thing that is supposed to tell us who we are. And inasmuch as we really are like what the perspective of technological capitalism tells us we are, then seeing ourselves through the lens of practices would seem like a needlessly complicated approach to the question of who we are. At best, it would serve as a baroque accessory to the real explanation, telling us a bit about some less important aspects of who we are, but not getting at the important point.

Having gone this far in looking at a single-explainer competitor to the practices approach in addressing the question of who we are, it remains to us only to ask how well this competitor stacks up against the approach with which I have extensively engaged you. Is the perspective of technological capitalism a better approach to who we are than the practices view is? Or does the practices view sustain its power in the face of technological capitalism? Ought we see ourselves primarily as participants in a diversity of ongoing practices, with their different values and knowledges and goals and power relations, or as consumers in a technologically advanced marketplace?

To address that question fully would take another book. Instead of writing that other book, and then attaching it to this one, let me instead just close with some passing thoughts. In doing philosophy, it is probably best not to try to answer all of the questions, but to leave the reader with some questions worth asking. And even if that's not the best, it's the best I can do. So instead of attempting to convince you of my own view in some final way, I'll just put a few thoughts forward for your consideration. You won't be surprised at what I'm about to say.

I believe that technological capitalism has indeed changed some of who we are, but that looking at practices remains the most important approach to answering that question. It would, of course, be silly to deny that the rise of technological capitalism and its diffusion throughout the world has not changed us. It has. Although I am uncomfortable with many of those changes, I'm willing to acknowledge that not all of them have been bad. The emergence of the Internet, for example, has in some ways made access to faraway places more democratic by offering us images and sounds and texts that might otherwise be reserved for those who can afford to travel to those places. In any case, for better and for worse, technological capitalism has altered our world in profound ways, and in doing so, has altered us.

But it's easy—too easy—to look at the grand scheme of things and conclude that that's all there is to see. If I am right in the case I've made for practices throughout this book, then much more of who we are happens on a local social level than grand schemes are likely to be able to capture. Our values, our inferential structures, and our daily engagements arise much more out of the structure and history of our practices than they do out of the overarching economic system to which we are subject. This is not to deny that the economic system has wrought changes in our daily practices. After all, I have emphasized that our practices are not given to us by cosmic forces beyond the reach of our history and our environment. They arise through history and in the context of various environmental influences. Technological capitalism, inasmuch as it has changed our history and our environment, affects our practices. But to think that those practices are so completely colonized as to be reducible to capitalist forces is to see our world from too high a bird's-eye view.

Unless and until technological capitalism—or some other force that can be summed up by a single-explainer theory—embeds itself so deeply into our practices that our knowledge, our values, and our daily lives look merely like reflections of it, the practices approach to who we are will continue to hold sway against it.

We are, I suspect, not nearly there yet. And, for reasons I have put before you over the course of our journey through these pages, we are unlikely to be there for some time to come.

BIBLIOGRAPHY

Appiah, Kwame Anthony. *In My Father's House: Africa in the Philosophy of Culture.* Oxford: Oxford University Press, 1992.

Brandom, Robert. *Making It Explicit: Reasoning, Representing, and Discursive Commitment.* Cambridge: Harvard University Press, 1994.

Descartes, René. *Meditations on First Philosophy.* Translated by Laurence Lafleur. Indianapolis: Bobbs-Merrill Co., 1951.

Dworkin, Ronald. *Taking Rights Seriously.* Cambridge: Harvard University Press, 1977.

Dyer, Geoff. *But Beautiful: A Book About Jazz.* New York: North Point Press, 1996.

Foucault, Michel. *Discipline and Punish: The Birth of the Prison.* Translated by Alan Sheridan. New York: Random House, 1977.

———. *The History of Sexuality.* Vol. 1, *An Introduction.* Translated by Robert Hurley. New York: Random House, 1978.

———. "The Subject and Power." Afterword to Hubert L. Dreyfus and Paul Rabinow, *Michel Foucault: Beyond Structuralism and Hermeneutics.* Chicago: University of Chicago Press, 1982.

Gadamer, Hans-Georg. *Truth and Method.* New York: Crossroad, 1975.

Gettier, Edmund. "Is Justified True Belief Knowledge?" *Analysis* 23 (1963), 121–23.

Grover, Dorothy; Joseph Camp, Jr.; and Nuel D. Belnap, Jr. "A Prosentential Theory of Truth." *Philosophical Studies* 27 (1975), 73–125.

Harris, Judith Rich. *The Nurture Assumption: Why Children Turn Out the Way They Do.* New York: Free Press, 1998.

Husserl, Edmund. *Cartesian Meditations: An Introduction to Phenomenology.* Translated by Dorion Cairns. The Hague: Martinus Nijhoff, 1977.

Kuhn, Thomas. *The Structure of Scientific Revolutions.* 2d ed. Chicago: University of Chicago Press, 1962.

Lyotard, Jean-François. *The Differend: Phrases in Dispute.* Translated by Georges Van Den Abbeele. Minneapolis: University of Minnesota Press, 1988.

Miyoshi, Masao. "A Borderless World? From Colonialism to Transnationalism and the Decline of the Nation-State." *Critical Inquiry* 19 (Summer 1993), 726–51.

Nagel, Thomas. *The View from Nowhere.* Oxford: Oxford University Press, 1986.

Putnam, Robert. "Bowling Alone: America's Declining Social Capital." *Journal of Democracy* 6, no. 1 (1995), 65–78.

Rouse, Joseph. *Engaging Science: How to Understand Its Practices Philosophically.* Ithaca: Cornell University Press, 1996.

Sandel, Michael J. *Liberalism and the Limits of Justice.* Cambridge: Cambridge University Press, 1982.

Sartre, Jean-Paul. *Being and Nothingness: A Phenomenological Essay on Ontology.* Translated by Hazel Barnes. New York: Philosophical Library, 1956.

Schatzki, Theodore R. *Social Practices: A Wittgensteinian Approach to Human Activity and the Social.* Cambridge: Cambridge University Press, 1996.

Wallace, James D. *Ethical Norms, Particular Cases.* Ithaca: Cornell University Press, 1996.

Wittgenstein, Ludwig. *On Certainty.* Translated by Denis Paul and G. E. M. Anscombe. London: Basil Blackwell, 1969.

———. *Philosophical Investigations.* 3d ed. Translated by G. E. M. Anscombe. London: Basil Blackwell, 1958.

INDEX

Made in the USA
Columbia, SC
18 June 2019